The Model of Open Cooperativism

Vangelis Papadimitropoulos

ANTHEM PRESS

Anthem Press
An imprint of Wimbledon Publishing Company
www.anthempress.com

This edition first published in UK and USA 2026
by ANTHEM PRESS
75–76 Blackfriars Road, London SE1 8HA, UK
or PO Box 9779, London SW19 7ZG, UK
and
244 Madison Ave #116, New York, NY 10016, USA

British Library Cataloguing-in-Publication Data
A catalogue record for this book is available from the British Library.

Library of Congress Cataloging-in-Publication Data: 2026939563

ISBN-13: 978-1-80136-099-9 (Pbk)
ISBN-10: 1-80136-099-5 (Pbk)

This title is also available as an eBook.

TABLE OF CONTENTS

1. Introduction 1

2. Merging Cooperatives with the Commons: The Model of Open Cooperativism 5

3. Envisioning the Post-Hegemony of Open Cooperativism 21

4. Methodology 29

5. Case Studies 31

6. Cross-Case Thematic Analysis and Discussion 53

7. Conclusion 57

References 63

Index 73

Chapter 1
INTRODUCTION

This book builds on the findings of a three-year research project titled "Techno-Social Innovation in the Collaborative Economy" to propose a novel socioeconomic model termed "open cooperativism." At its core, open cooperativism aims to unite the commons with cooperative modes of production, effectively merging Elinor Ostrom's design principle of nested enterprises with the traditional cooperative principle of intercooperation among cooperatives. Ostrom used the concept of nested enterprises to describe public–private–commons partnerships involved in the maintenance and provision of common-pool resources such as forests, irrigation fields, pastures, and fisheries. Later, scholars expanded the Ostromian framework in urban commons. In the model of open cooperativism, the digital commons add up to rural and urban commons to serve as a critical link facilitating collaboration between these distinct yet complementary organizational forms. Ultimately, open cooperativism aims to foster strong synergies among multiple stakeholders—including civil society organizations, ethical market actors, cooperatives, and supportive state institutions—working collectively toward an ethical, inclusive, and sustainable postcapitalist economy.

Recent decades have witnessed the rapid ascent of digital economy models enabled by transformative Internet technologies, including platform capitalism, platform cooperativism, peer production, and the digital commons. Platform capitalism thrives on leveraging network effects through digital platforms to create multi-sided markets and facilitate trade, predominantly driven by profit maximization and investor ownership. In stark contrast, platform cooperativism integrates traditional cooperative principles—such as democratic governance, collective ownership, and equitable distribution—into digital infrastructures. This creates cooperative-owned digital platforms designed to prioritize social, ethical, and ecological objectives rather than purely commercial imperatives. Platform cooperatives, thus, represent viable alternatives capable of addressing the shortcomings of capitalist-driven platform models by fostering ethical economic engagement, fair labor conditions, and sustainability.

However, despite their transformative potential, platform cooperatives face several structural limitations, including difficulties in achieving economies of scale, accessing capital, navigating regulatory landscapes, and resisting pressures toward demutualization. To address these limitations and further enhance cooperative impact, Michel Bauwens and Vasilis Kostakis advocate transforming platform cooperativism into "open cooperativism" by embedding commons-based peer production at the core into cooperative practice. Open cooperativism builds upon the foundational ideas of platform cooperativism while emphasizing openness, transparency, and the production and sharing of commons within and beyond cooperative boundaries. This approach seeks a holistic transition towards a commons-oriented, sustainable, and regenerative socioeconomic system.

To empirically explore these concepts, the book employs a multi-case study approach, examining six exemplary initiatives—P2P Lab/Tzoumakers in Greece, Open Food Network (OFN) internationally, CoopCycle in France, and Circles UBI in Germany, as well as Subvert and Transkribus internationally—that implement elements of commons-based peer production and open cooperativism. Commons-based peer production emerges from decentralized collaboration within open-source software communities and the digital commons and connects with traditional cooperative organizations in the model of open cooperativism.

Tzoumakers leverages open-source hardware and software to develop agricultural tools locally through a cosmolocal production model, empowering small-scale farmers and enhancing community resilience. The Open Food Network builds decentralized, transparent short food supply chains, strengthening producer–consumer relationships and ecological sustainability. CoopCycle confronts exploitative gig-economy practices by creating a federated network of bike-delivery cooperatives employing ethical digital platforms. Finally, Circles UBI uses blockchain technology to pioneer a decentralized mutual credit system, providing universal basic income tokens intended to stimulate local economies and promote socioeconomic equity. Subvert offers a replicable framework for collectively owned digital marketplaces, focusing on the music industry and artist empowerment, while Transkribus, operated by READ-COOP SCE, exemplifies platform cooperativism in the field of artificial intelligence (AI)-driven cultural heritage, providing cooperative governance for automated text recognition and digital commons in the archival sector.

By critically analyzing these case studies, the book highlights how commons-based digital resources and cooperative governance models can facilitate diverse forms of socioeconomic organization aligned with open cooperativism. It also identifies the substantial challenges each initiative encounters concerning economic sustainability, governance structures, scalability, regulatory ambiguities, and tensions between commons-driven values and market realities. In doing so, the book not only assesses the strengths and limitations of these grassroots models but also proposes a cohesive theoretical and practical roadmap for integrating platform cooperativism and commons-based peer production within the broader sociopolitical landscape. Ultimately, the research contributes toward fostering stronger intercooperation among commons-producing civil society entities, ethical market organizations, and supportive state institutions, guiding collective efforts toward a genuinely post-capitalist, inclusive, and sustainable economic future.

The book is structured as follows:

In Chapter 2, *Merging Cooperatives with the Commons: The Model of Open Cooperativism*, the book introduces the theoretical foundation of open cooperativism. It explores key concepts such as commons-based peer production, cosmolocalism, and the transition from platform cooperativism to open cooperativism. Drawing on the work of Elinor Ostrom, Michel Bauwens, and Vasilis Kostakis, this chapter defines how digital commons and cooperative structures can merge to create an alternative economic model that fosters sustainability, inclusivity, and ethical governance.

In Chapter 3, *Envisioning the Post-Hegemony of Open Cooperativism*, the discussion moves to the broader political and economic implications of open cooperativism. This chapter examines how open cooperativism can function as a counter-hegemonic force against platform capitalism. It discusses the roles of ethical market entities, civil society organizations, and a "partner state" in fostering a post-capitalist transition. The chapter also highlights systemic obstacles, including economic pressures, regulatory constraints, and the need for institutional support.

In Chapter 4, *Methodology*, the book outlines the research approach, detailing the multi-case study methodology used to analyze the selected initiatives. It describes data collection techniques such as interviews, literature reviews, and participatory observation. Additionally, the chapter explains the thematic coding strategy applied to assess governance, economic models, legal frameworks, and challenges within the case studies.

In Chapter 5, *Case Studies*, the book presents six in-depth case studies that exemplify open cooperativism in practice. Each case study is analyzed through the lenses of four thematic codes: (1) value proposition; (2) governance; (3) economic model; and (4) legal structure:

- **P2P Lab/Tzoumakers (Greece):** A cosmolocalism-based initiative that uses open-source hardware to develop agricultural tools for small-scale farmers.

- **Open Food Network (Australia):** A decentralized platform enabling short food supply chains that eliminate intermediaries and strengthen local food systems.
- **CoopCycle (France):** A federation of bike delivery cooperatives that leverage digital commons to counteract exploitative gig-economy models.
- **Circles UBI (Germany):** A blockchain-based universal basic income (UBI) system that fosters alternative monetary ecosystems and economic self-sufficiency.
- **Subvert (US):** A collectively owned digital marketplace that applies cooperativist principles to the cultural and creative industries.
- **Transkribus (Austria):** An AI-driven text recognition and transcription platform operated by READ-COOP SCE, which exemplifies platform and open cooperativism in the cultural heritage sector through cooperative governance of digital commons and shared technological infrastructure.

In Chapter 6, *Cross-Case Thematic Analysis and Discussion*, the book synthesizes the findings from the case studies into four key thematic areas:

- **Value Proposition:** Examines how these initiatives generate economic, social, and environmental value by integrating commons-based peer production with cooperative structures.
- **Governance:** Analyzes governance structures, including multi-stakeholder participation, decentralization, and decision-making processes across the initiatives.
- **Economy:** Investigates financial sustainability, revenue models, and the balance between commons-based production and market viability.
- **Law:** Explores the legal frameworks that support or hinder these initiatives, including licensing models, intellectual property rights, and regulatory challenges.

In Chapter 7, *Conclusion*, the book summarizes the key insights gained from the research, reflecting on the strengths and limitations of open cooperativism. It provides recommendations for policymakers, cooperative practitioners, and researchers interested in advancing the commons-based economy. The book concludes with a call for sustained intercooperation and policy innovation to support the transition toward a post-capitalist, inclusive, and sustainable economic framework.

Chapter 2

MERGING COOPERATIVES WITH THE COMMONS: THE MODEL OF OPEN COOPERATIVISM

2.1. Commons-based Peer Production

Recent decades have witnessed a significant "paradigm shift" (Kuhn 1962) within market economies, driven by three central forces: (1) advancements in information and communication technologies (ICTs); (2) climate change; and (3) the rise of platform economics. ICTs, with attributes such as cost efficiency, networked infrastructure, decentralization, modularity, and open-sourcing (Bauwens et al. 2019; Castells 2011), combined with sustainability-driven transformations (Kallis 2018; Markard et al. 2012; Ostrom 1990), and peer production (Bauwens et al. 2019; Benkler 2006), have catalyzed innovative organizational structures characterized by varied production methods and labor types within the digital economy.

This evolution has concurrently given rise to post-Fordism (Hardt and Negri 2000), neoliberalism (Brown 2015), the Californian ideology (Smyrnaios 2018), open-source software/hardware movements (Benkler 2006), and digital commons (Aigrain 2012; Griffiths 2008; Morell 2010; Stalder 2010). It has also facilitated crowdsourcing (Howe 2006) and various types of immaterial or digital labor (Hardt and Negri 2004; Fuchs 2014; Scholz 2016), performed by the multitude (Hardt and Negri 2004), the cyber-precariat (Dyer-Witherford 2015; Standing 2011; Huws 2003, 2014), prosumers (Toffler 1980), and e-communities (Fuchs 2014). In essence, digital capitalism (Fuchs 2022) intersects with peer production at the nexus of online and offline, blending both commercial and non-commercial forms of activity.

Peer production refers broadly to decentralized, collaborative efforts among peers leveraging the Internet and its network effects and shared resources, including knowledge, software, and designs, to create outcomes oriented toward the commons. This approach emphasizes openness, collective creation, self-management, and social innovation. Instances of peer production include peer-to-peer networks, free/libre and open-source software (FLOSS), and digital platforms. By supporting diverse identities and digital communities, peer production engages sociopolitical trends and ideologies such as techno-feudalism (Varoufakis 2023), libertarianism, post-politics (Crouch 2004), and populism (Laclau 2005), positioning itself uniquely at the intersection of neoliberal globalization (Brown 2015) and the commodification of the Internet (Papadimitropoulos 2022; Smyrnaios 2018).

Consequently, peer production has supported the development of novel organizational forms such as platform capitalism (Srnicek 2017), FLOSS (Stallman 2002), the digital commons (Benkler 2006), platform cooperativism (Scholz 2016), cosmolocalism (Bauwens et al. 2019), Distributed Autonomous Organizations (DAOs) utilizing blockchain technology (De Filippi et al. 2024), and open cooperativism (Papadimitropoulos 2020).

The literature (Benkler 2006; Kostakis and Bauwens 2014; Papadimitropoulos 2019, 2022; Scholz 2016; Troxler 2010) has documented two primary instances of peer production: (1) firm-hosted peer production, or platform capitalism, also referred to as the sharing and gig economy, employing user-centered innovation and crowdsourcing models; and (2) commons-based peer production, encompassing platform cooperatives, open cooperatives, digital and local commons, DAOs, and the Design Global-Manufacture Local (DGML) model.

Firm-hosted peer production primarily aims at maximizing profits by centrally leveraging user-generated knowledge, digital communities, and online labor (Fuchs 2014), as exemplified by companies like Facebook, Google, Amazon, Microsoft, and Alibaba. This corporate subsumption of peer production capitalizes on network effects, first-mover advantages, economies of scale, and lock-in effects, consolidating significant market power within platform capitalism (Srnicek 2017). Today's platform capitalism increasingly aligns with authoritarian and neoconservative populist ideologies, perpetuating the enclosure of knowledge, intensifying inequalities, creating power imbalances, erecting barriers to new market entrants, stifling innovation, and limiting meaningful digital participation.

Platform capitalism operates within a global economic landscape characterized by disruptive technological innovations driven by ongoing digitalization, clashing with the headwinds of persistent market failures and inefficiencies. Extensive research (Benanav 2020; Brynjolfsson and McAfee 2014; Lapavitsas 2022; Stiglitz 2012; Summers 2014) identifies systemic flaws inherent in capitalist economies, including market failures like information asymmetries, adverse selection, missing markets, moral hazard, and credit rationing. Supply-side issues such as inadequate investment in infrastructure and innovation, market monopolies and monopsonies, and price and wage rigidity further weaken these systems (Stiglitz 2012). Concurrently, demand-side problems and inefficient resource allocation contribute to economic stagnation, sluggish productivity, and inadequate investment—elements collectively described as "secular stagnation" (Summers 2014). Secular stagnation intensifies social and economic disparities, heightens political tensions, and worsens environmental crises, exacerbated further by global challenges such as pandemics, geopolitical conflicts, trade wars, inflation, and disrupted supply chains.

Conversely, commons-based peer production leverages grassroots, Internet-driven innovation and cooperative models to cultivate a more inclusive, equitable, and sustainable economy. This mode of production emphasizes decentralized ownership and self-governance structures (Benkler 2006; Scholz 2016). Historically, the concept of the "commons" traces back to collective ownership in primitive societies, Aristotle's republican ideals, feudal commons, and modern political philosophies (Fourier 1971; Marx 1857/1858; Owen 1991; Proudhon 1994). Today, the commons involve decentralized resources and infrastructure—such as natural resources, software/hardware, knowledge, information, and capital—self-managed by communities according to mutually agreed-upon rules and norms (Bollier and Helfrich 2012). Commons can range from local resources to digital infrastructures, including natural resources, software/hardware, knowledge, information, and capital (Hess and Ostrom 2007).

Digital commons, specifically, consist of open-source software, the Internet, blockchain technology, and hardware resources such as computer numerical control machines and 3D printers. The digital commons refers to a non-market sector of information, knowledge and cultural production, not treated as private property but as an ethic of sharing, self-management, and cooperation within peers who have open access to the Internet and free/open source software (Benkler 2006). The digital commons present an alternative to traditional models of intellectual property by promoting open access, collaborative innovation, and knowledge sharing. In doing so, they alleviate barriers to information, encourage community ownership, and contribute to knowledge democratization, fostering more inclusive, sustainable digital ecosystems.

Commons-based peer production leverages decentralized collaboration, open-source innovation, and community-driven governance, giving rise to novel organizational models such as cosmolocalism, platform cooperatives, open cooperatives, and Distributed Autonomous Organizations (DAOs). Blockchain-based digital commons, in particular, have diverse applications, including e-voting, e-governance, supply chain management, and collaborative finance, offering new organizational structures and facilitating decentralized cooperation (Papadimitropoulos 2022).

The literature identifies three primary normative approaches to commons-based peer production (Papadimitropoulos 2020): a liberal approach (Benkler 2006; Lessig 2001, 2004; Murdock 2013; Ostrom 1990), a reformist/post-capitalist approach (Arvidsson and Peitersen 2013; Bollier and Helfrich 2012, 2015; Kostakis and Bauwens 2014; Rifkin 2014; Rushkoff 2016; Scholz 2016; Wright 2009), and a radical approach (Caffentzis 2014; De Angelis 2018; Dardot and Laval 2014; Federici 2012; Fuchs 2014; Gibson and Graham 2006; Hardt and Negri 2009; Kioupkiolis 2019; Rigi 2014). The liberal view supports the coexistence of commons alongside state and market mechanisms. The reformist/post-capitalist perspective promotes transforming capitalism into a commons-oriented post-capitalism. Meanwhile, the radical anti-capitalist stance emphasizes the commons' autonomy from the capitalist state-market system. However, this categorization is schematic and avoids simplistic ideological labeling since arguments frequently overlap across these viewpoints.

Liberal scholars conceive of the commons as an alternative mode of production that exists alongside liberal democracy and the capitalist market. The commons pertain to the civil society that interacts both with privatization and government regulation. Liberal scholars such as Elinor Ostrom (1990, 2000), Lawrence Lessig (2001, 2004), and Yochai Benkler (2006, 2013) envisage the future of the commons in tandem with the state-market operation. With the exceptions of some anarchistic and collectivist strands, the liberal commons by large do not intend to challenge the state-capitalism nexus but to coexist peacefully on the premises of civil society, the state, and the capitalist market.

Reformist scholars approach the commons as an alternative organizational model of civil society, economy, and politics, which does not necessarily oppose liberal democracy and the capitalist market, nor does it peacefully coexist with them. Reformists such as Bauwens and Kostakis (2019), Bollier (2003, 2008, 2014), Rushkoff (2016), and Olin Wright (2009), among others, seek to transform the state-capitalism nexus by advancing the commons into a dominant mode of production that is increasingly less dependent on corporations and state intervention. The reformist approach of the commons combines liberal, social democratic, socialist, and revolutionary elements in varying forms to foster a commons-based transition toward a postcapitalist ethical and sustainable economy.

Anti-capitalist thinkers champion the commons as an anti-capitalist terrain of production that clashes head-on with capitalism and the state. For anti-capitalists, the commons engages in a constant class struggle with capitalism (Papadimitropoulos 2017: 572). Well-renowned scholars such as Ernesto Laclau and Chantal Mouffe (2001), Pierre Dardot and Christian

Laval (2014, 2017), Massimo De Angelis (2017), George Caffentzis (2014), Silvia Federici (2004, 2012), and Alexandros Kioupkiolis (2017, 2021, 2023) set out from a radical standpoint to confront neoliberal capitalism and render the commons autonomous vis-à-vis the state-capitalism nexus. All oppose the concept of a "liberal commons," that is, a commons confined to civil society that operates at the fringes of market economy and the state.

2.2. From Traditional Commons to the Digital Commons and Platform Cooperativism

Elinor Ostrom (1990), who received the Nobel Prize in Economics in 2009, extensively studied successful self-managed common-pool resources such as forests, pastures, fisheries, and irrigation fields. Yochai Benkler (2006) coined the term "commons-based peer production" to describe a sector of information, knowledge, and cultural production that functions outside traditional market structures. Instead of relying on private property, commons-based peer production embodies values of sharing, self-management, and cooperative engagement among peers with open access to the Internet and free/open-source software. Digital commons represent an institutional model for accessing, using, and controlling resources that significantly deviates from hierarchical and market-based structures. Key characteristics of digital commons include: (1) decentralized self-governance through participatory, meritocratic (do-ocratic), and charismatic models rather than proprietary or contractual ones; (2) prioritization of non-monetary incentives; and (3) permeability across state and corporate boundaries (Benkler 2006). Commons-based peer production thus introduces innovative forms of ownership, governance, operations, and finance, empowering communities against prevalent economic inequalities and power disparities. Notable examples include Wikipedia, Slashdot, Loomio, Drupal, Linux, Apache, Mozilla, WordPress, LibreOffice, among numerous others.

Jeremy Rifkin (2014) presents a model of green capitalism interconnected with the Internet of Things infrastructure, powered by renewable energy and open-source technology, envisioning a gradual transition toward Collaborative Commons. Trebor Scholz (2016) enhances the notion of Collaborative Commons through platform cooperativism, positioned as an alternative to platform capitalism (the prevalent sharing and gig economy). Platform cooperativism promotes online business structures where algorithms and digital platforms support democratic governance, collective ownership, and equitable value distribution. Prominent instances of platform cooperativism include Stocksy, the Drivers Cooperative, Loconomics, Transkribus, CoopCycle, Cobudget, among others.

2.3. Cosmolocalism

Vasilis Kostakis and Michel Bauwens (2014) propose bridging the gap between Ostrom's concept of local commons and Benkler's idea of global digital commons through commons-based peer production integrated with the Design Global-Manufacture Local (DG-ML) model, or cosmolocalism. Enabled by the combination of open-source software and accessible desktop manufacturing technologies (e.g., 3D printing, CNC machines), cosmolocalism establishes a model where globally abundant resources—such as knowledge, designs, and software—remain universally accessible, while locally scarce resources, primarily hardware, are managed and produced within communities.

Through cosmolocalism, global digital commons are effectively linked to decentralized urban and rural communities, makerspaces, and fablabs powered by renewable energy systems interconnected via microgrids, the Internet of Things (IoT), and blockchain technologies. This approach democratizes the design and production processes, enabling communities, prosumers, social enterprises, cooperatives, and civil society organizations to collaboratively access, modify, and share knowledge globally while fabricating products locally according to specific needs.

Artifacts produced under the DG-ML model transcend traditional commodity status by functioning as shared commons. Cosmolocalism thus significantly reduces production costs, enhances communication, and fosters greater user interaction, promoting beneficial network effects and grassroots social innovation. It prioritizes cooperation over competition, openness over intellectual property restrictions, circular economies over planned obsolescence, and advocates for post-growth or degrowth models as opposed to conventional green-growth frameworks. In short, open cooperatives models such as cosmolocalism variously dissociate from neoclassical economics in terms of normative assumptions, value theory, property rights, governance, division of labor, and incentives (Table 2.1).

> The DG-ML model emphasizes application that is small-scale, decentralized, resilient and locally controlled. In other words, a model of sustainable development which recognizes the limits to growth posed by finite resources and organizes material activities accordingly (Kostakis et al. 2015: 131).

Cosmolocalism introduces a simple yet transformative concept: significant improvements in production and management can be achieved through the glocal sharing of resources, knowledge, and power. Rigid intellectual

Table 2.1. Neoclassical vs Cooperative Economics

	Neoclassical economics	**Cooperative economics**
Assumptions	Scarcity, market forces, price mechanism, perfect competition, pareto-optimal allocation of resources	Cooperation, openness, sharing, scarcity, and abundance
Incentives	Profit motive, individualism	Diversity of incentives, individuality and collectivity, mutualism
Value theory	Marginal utility theory, exchange value, commodification	Collective sense making, use value, individual, and social needs
Property rights	Private property rights, intellectual property rights	Bundle of private and common-property rights (access, withdrawal, management, exclusion, alienation)
Economic model	Capitalism, green growth, eco-efficiency, economies of scale	Postcapitalism, degrowth/post-growth, eco-sufficiency, economies of scope

property rights often lead to underutilization and inefficient use of knowledge (Arrow 1962; Stiglitz 2008). However, combining private property rights with common property rights such as access, withdrawal, and comanagement can facilitate innovative governance (Schlager and Ostrom 1992). Principles of sharing, openness, transparency, and self-management foster a continuously evolving collective repository of optimal practices, ideas, knowledge, and resources, accessible and contributable by various stakeholders based on their specific needs and capabilities (Bauwens et al. 2019; Benkler 2006; Bollier and Helfrich 2015; Ostrom 1990). In this model, market exchange value (scarcity) complements the use value provided by the digital commons (abundance), addressing social needs instead of perpetuating consumerism, extractivism, and productivism, which negatively impact society and the environment.

Examples of DG-ML initiatives such as L'Atelier Paysan, OpenBionics, Sensorica, Wikihouse, RepRap, and FarmHack illustrate the potential of leveraging digital commons to engage a global community for project development. These cases demonstrate how integrating digital commons with local manufacturing technologies can enhance individual and collective autonomy and transform various production sectors toward sustainability and social innovation (Gershenfeld 2007; Kostakis et al. 2016). Unlike traditional large-scale industrial manufacturing, DG-ML emphasizes small-scale, decentralized, resilient, and community-controlled applications. Kostakis et al. (2015, 2016, 2023) argue that DG-ML recognizes finite resource constraints and organizes material production activities accordingly. Viewed as a niche practice, DG-ML might serve as a source of innovative solutions for current societal tensions or even act as a model for broader systemic transformation (Smith 2007).

2.4. From Platform Cooperatives to Open Cooperativism

Cooperatives today are a significant part of the global economy. According to the International Labor Organization and International Co-operative Alliance (2014), there are approximately three million cooperatives worldwide, with an estimated one billion members. These cooperatives operate across a wide range of sectors, including agriculture, finance, healthcare, housing, and retail.

Technological change in the last decades has spurred the formation of a new type of cooperative termed "platform cooperative" that adapts traditional cooperative principles to the digital economy, specifically to online platforms (Scholz 2016; Scholz and Schneider 2016). Trebor Scholz (2016) has coined the term "platform cooperativism" to describe an Internet-enabled model of production where digital platforms are communally shared and run by their members. A common definition of a platform cooperative is the following one:

> A platform cooperative, or platform co-op, is a cooperatively owned, democratically governed business that establishes a computing platform, and uses a website, mobile app or a protocol to facilitate the sale of goods and services (Calzada 2020, 8).

Scholz et al. (2021, 15) define a platform cooperative as "worker co-ops, data co-ops, multi-stakeholder co-ops, and producer co-ops for whom their digital business is central to their operation." Another plausible definition of a platform cooperative would describe "an enterprise that operates primarily through digital platforms for interaction or the exchange of goods and/or services and is structured in line with the International Cooperative Alliance Statement on the Cooperative Identity" (Mayo 2019, 20).

Platform cooperatives are formed and operated by the users, workers, or stakeholders via an online platform, such as a website or app. The idea is to use the algorithmic design of profit-driven platforms such as Uber and Airbnb in the service of a cooperative business model based on community ownership, democratic governance, sustainability, and fair distribution of value (Scholz 2016, 2023). The aim is to create a more equitable model in contrast to traditional tech platforms like Uber or Amazon, where control and profits are centralized in the hands of a few investors or founders. Instead of workers earning meagre wages from precarious labor that makes investors rich, they would be able to design, manage, and own the means of production themselves.

Platform cooperativism works on the model of a multi-stakeholder synergy of consumers, investors, producers, and users. It aims to reunite existing cooperatives and labor unions under digital self-governance. Among several examples of platform cooperatives, there are the ride-hailing cooperative, The Drivers Cooperative, and the remote teachers' cooperative, MyCoolClass. Currently, 638 projects that could classify under the term "platform cooperative" span 53 countries.[1]

More recently, "data cooperatives" have also come into the picture. These are democratically controlled structures that "enable the creation of open data and personal data stores for mutual benefit," in an effort to ameliorate the asymmetries that exist between data subjects and organizations that collect, process, and use their data (Mannan et al. 2022, 12). Data cooperatives are not only intended to help users, workers, and other stakeholders control access to their data, but also create new ways for vulnerable groups to use their personal and collective data for commercial and noncommercial ends, as well as collective bargaining with data processing entities. Data cooperatives like Salus enable patients to share their medical data with healthcare institutions on their own terms, while the Driver's Seat Cooperative helped ride-hailing drivers to collect and analyze data about their trips on ride-hailing platforms, thereby enhancing their bargaining position relative to large corporate platforms like Uber and Lyft (Mannan et al. 2022; Micheli et al. 2023).

Platform cooperatives like the Drivers Cooperative, MyCoolClass, Salus, CoopCycle, Transkribus, and others have emerged in response to mounting concerns over excessive workplace surveillance, erosion of privacy, opaque algorithmic management, and the precarious nature of gig work. At the same time, they confront broader systemic challenges such as concentrated ownership, diminishing labor rights, and the disproportionate political power of tech giants.

Yet, to the degree that cooperatives strive for holistic socioeconomic change, the cooperative movement is still far from challenging the current capitalist status quo. The largest 300 cooperatives and mutuals reported a combined turnover exceeding two trillion USD, based on 2017 financial data (International Cooperative Alliance and Euricse 2023). In certain countries,

1 https://directory.platform.coop/#1/31.1/-84.8

cooperatives contribute significantly to the national gross domestic product (GDP) (New Zealand: 20%, Netherlands: 18%, France: 18%, Finland: 14%, Spain: 10%, Italy: 7%). Given that the global GDP was approximately $85.8 trillion in 2018, the turnover of the top 300 cooperatives represents a substantial economic force (International Labour Organization 2022). Despite these figures, the cooperative sector's share remains relatively modest compared to the dominant capitalist sector.

2.5. Cooperativism Through and Beyond Standard Economic Theory

Conventional economic theory—particularly neoclassical theory, neo-institutional economics, property rights theory, and agency theory—often analyze cooperatives as anomalies or exceptions to the dominant investor-owned firm (IOF) model. Cooperatives are treated as inefficient organizational types whose presence is typically transient and of some importance in times of crises and to marginal socioeconomic participants (Altman 2010). Cooperatives are considered to be emerging primarily in response to incomplete and missing markets (Hueth 2014). Cooperatives often appear when the regular market doesn't work well—for example, when people can't get fair prices, basic services, or access to important goods. If businesses or the government aren't meeting a need, people sometimes join together to create a cooperative and solve the problem themselves. So, cooperatives are a way for communities to fill gaps where the market is missing or unfair.

Neo-institutional economics regards cooperatives as specialized entities that arise to address market failures such as monopolies, monopsonies, multi-stakeholder partnerships, or situations involving homogeneous membership. If one company controls all the buying or selling (a monopoly or monopsony), or if many different groups need to work together, cooperatives can help fix the situation. They're especially useful when the members have similar goals or needs, so they can manage things more effectively as a group.

In short, co-ops are a tool to overcome deficiencies of a not-yet-mature market. They fill a gap, but when markets are fully functioning, there are no important gaps any longer and co-ops are no longer necessary. Eventually, market forces—technological change, supply and demand dynamics, individual preferences, competition over scarce resources, the use of prices as indicators of scarcity, and the profit motive—are the sole drivers of economic activity.

Moreover, cooperatives inevitably face financial, incentive, and coordination issues. The under-capitalization and under-investment thesis (Furubotn and Pejovich 1970) argues that the growth of co-ops is constrained by their limited access to fresh capital; co-ops cannot offer new shares on the stock exchange like (listed) IOFs—where expected future profit flows could otherwise increase share value for members. Ill-defined or non-tradable ownership rights in co-ops make capital accumulation and control less efficient.

Cooperatives are risk-averse (the portfolio problem) and, therefore, have limited success since they are not obliged to invest profits (focusing on employment and workers' income). Members tend to keep investments low because the target of cooperatives was to maximize the income of current members while keeping returns on capital as low as possible (Vanek 1977; Ward 1958). Members tend to privilege strategies maximizing returns over the short term of their expected presence in the cooperative, because they are in no position to cash the capital gains on the shares when they leave (the horizon problem).

Collective governance (the decision problem) over heterogeneous membership can be slow and conflict-ridden due to members having different financial goals and risk tolerances. Classic principal-agent problems—such as moral hazard—arise since the monitoring of managers by members is more complex due to collective ownership. In case commitment of members is no longer granted, a free-rider problem may occur. New members can often access benefits without making equal investments. Since a minimum investment is enough to obtain voting rights, further investment may be withheld by some (Battilani and Schröter 2012). Co-ops are thus too egalitarian to generate economically efficient incentives and to engage the employment of superior management.

Incentive and coordination problems raise the cost of contracting and control in cooperatives compared to investor-owned firms. Because ownership is shared and motivation is often diverse, cooperatives face structural challenges in sustaining long-term efficiency and engagement. Cooperatives reduce contracting costs by internalizing relationships (e.g., between workers and firms, or producers and processors), but they may incur higher ownership costs due to democratic governance, consensus-building, and collective decision-making.

IOFs dominate because they operate with clear property rights, aligned incentives, and homogeneity of interests, while benefiting from efficient capital markets that enable them to bear risk for long-term investments. As a result, they are structurally well-suited to capital-intensive, scalable, and competitive markets—especially under prevailing institutional and legal systems.

Despite the structural weaknesses of coops, a substantial body of empirical research and theoretical advancements have demonstrated their capacity for growth, financial stability, and competitive performance (Dow 2003;

Fakhfakh et al. 2012; Jensen and McDonnell 2019; Spear 2000). These findings underscore the potential of cooperatives as a sustainable and equitable component of the modern economy. A major component of the sustainability of co-ops is their comparative advantage vis-à-vis IOFs such as their social mission, resilience, employment stability, transparency, and pooling of resources, among others.

However, while the cooperative movement has successfully built strong local solidarity networks in countries like Italy, France, Spain, Canada, and India, the application of the sixth cooperative principle—intercooperation among cooperatives—remains limited on a global scale. This is particularly noticeable as cooperatives grow into larger, often transnational organizations such as Mondragon and several major Italian multinational co-ops, as well as cooperative banks and insurance companies operating internationally (Restakis 2010).

Growth and the pressures of accessing capital often lead large cooperatives toward demutualization, resulting in a gradual detachment from their original membership base and local communities. As these cooperatives become more market-oriented, their political and social missions are frequently sidelined, weakening their cooperative identity. Many large cooperatives are reluctant to share branding, marketing resources, and collaborative platforms with smaller cooperatives. Consequently, instead of strengthening a unified cooperative movement, these larger cooperatives risk absorption into the capitalist economy, sometimes transitioning into private, profit-oriented enterprises (Ben-Ner 1984; Miyazaki 1984). This trend is particularly visible in the agricultural sectors of Canada and Ireland in recent years (Restakis 2010).

Such dynamics have intensified polarization and inequality within the cooperative sector. A significant cultural and economic divide now exists between established, large-scale cooperatives and smaller, innovative, and emerging cooperatives. These smaller- and medium-sized cooperatives, despite their progressive ideas and practices, frequently encounter significant challenges, including limited access to capital, inadequate training opportunities, and a lack of entrepreneurial and managerial capacity. Additionally, institutional support from governments, larger cooperatives, and NGOs often remains insufficient. Small co-ops frequently find themselves isolated by the unwillingness of larger organizations and existing cooperative "gated communities" to engage in genuine collaboration.

Overall, both traditional and platform cooperatives come with a number of shortcomings such as difficulty in accessing capital and achieving economies of scale, limited market control, slow decision-making, low member involvement, mismanagement, demutualization, and opportunism

(Birchall and Ketilson 2009; De Lautour and Cortese 2016; Malta et al. 2020; Mannan and Pek 2024; Mohamad et al. 2013; Restakis 2010). Externally, cooperatives confront uneasy exits from IOFs due to path dependencies, lock-ins, vested interests, and high switching costs (Papadimitropoulos 2020). Finally, cooperatives have to encounter the lack of a regulatory framework proper for platform cooperatives and a relevant culture and education system (Davis 2001; Scholz 2016, 2023).

Not only do platform cooperatives have to address the shortcomings of traditional cooperatives, they also encounter the overall tendency of platform capitalism toward monopoly formation (Srnicek 2017). Platform cooperativism exhibits contradictions between politics and enterprise, democracy and the market, commons and commercialization, as well as activism and entrepreneurship (Sandoval 2020).

> "Platform cooperativism is proposing a bottom-up strategy of transforming platform capitalism. It seems promising as it offers an avenue for positive critique—a strategy of actively creating alternative realities instead of merely criticising existing ones. Such a bottom-up strategy is particularly appealing in times when many have lost confidence in neoliberal governments to regulate corporate power and support projects for social change. Many examples show that platform co-operatives can have positive impacts on their members and communities. However, thus far they have been unable to create large-scale structural change" (Sandoval 2020, 809).

Cooperatives ultimately face the challenge of balancing their dual nature—pursuing a social mission while achieving economic viability. Workers are often required to act as entrepreneurs, aligning their individual goals with the collective interests of the community (Bunders and De Moor 2024). While democratic governance is a core principle, the efficiency of hierarchical management may sometimes take precedence over slower, participatory decision-making processes. Similarly, maintaining a niche identity or "alternative" ethos can conflict with the need to go mainstream and achieve critical mass. Moreover, the autonomy of cooperatives is frequently shaped—and sometimes constrained—by market dynamics and policy environments.

Tensions and contradictions are detrimental to the overall transformative potential of the cooperative sector. Trebor Scholz (2016) himself oscillates between a moderate and a radical thesis when he contends that it is unrealistic to anticipate that platform co-ops will dominate capitalist markets, thus settling with a more diversified economy.

Overall, the literature has documented three basic normative approaches of the potential evolution of platform cooperativism vis-à-vis platform capitalism:

- The liberal regulation of platform capitalism towards an eco-friendly, social, and human digital capitalism (Codagnone et al. 2016a, 2016b; Eurofound 2018; Frenken et al. 2020; Rani et al. 2021; UNCTAD 2019).
- The reformist regulation of platform capitalism through democratization and/or nationalization (Dufresne and Leterme 2021; Fuchs 2014; Graham and Shaw 2017; Huws et al. 2017; Morozov 2018; Srnicek 2017; Joyce et al. 2023; Varoufakis 2020).
- The radical bottom-up replacement of platform capitalism with grassroots commons-based post-capitalist organizational models aided or not by the state (Bauwens et al. 2019; Fuster Morell and Espelt, 2018; Gibson-Graham 1996, 2006; Muldoon 2022; Papadimitropoulos 2020, 2022; Scholz 2016; van Doorn 2019; Woodcock 2020). This tendency often comes in terms of a radical reformism that seeks to create public service Internet platforms and platform coop/public service Internet hybrids that challenge the power of digital capitalism and aim at replacing it (Fuchs 2022).

Michel Bauwens and Vasilis Kostakis (2014, 2019) are exploring the third scenario of transforming platform cooperativism into open cooperativism. They integrate the concept of cosmolocalism into open cooperativism. Unlike traditional cooperatives and platform cooperatives—which typically operate under closed proprietary licenses and primarily share resources internally—open cooperatives aim to generate and distribute commons both internally and externally. They utilize open design principles, freely accessible information, and shared knowledge to establish a commons-based network economy. Within this framework, the abundance provided by the commons complements the scarcity inherent to post-capitalist markets, enabling diverse actors to sustainably access and replenish resources based on their unique needs and capacities.

The literature (Bauwens et al. 2019; Bauwens and Niaros 2017; Freund and Stanko 2018; Giotitsas and Ramos 2017) has identified a three-zone structure for open cooperativism consisting of: (1) civil society organizations generating material or immaterial commons; (2) ethical market entities creating exchange value in addition to the commons' use value; and (3) a supportive partner state (Pazaitis and Drechsler 2021) fostering public–private–commons partnerships. Examples illustrating the open cooperative model include initiatives such as Sensorica, Smart, and Enspiral, which span diverse fields such as creative and cultural industries, as well as software and hardware development (Bauwens and Niaros 2017; Bauwens and Pantazis 2018; Pazaitis et al. 2017).

Open cooperatives implement open protocols, internalize negative externalities, adopt multi-stakeholder governance structures, actively contribute to the development of both tangible and intangible commons, and pursue global socioeconomic and political transformations rooted in local communities (Table 2.2).

Table 2.2. From the capitalist enterprise to an open cooperative

	Investor-owned enterprise	**Traditional cooperative**	**Open cooperative**
Ownership, legal entity	Shareholder ownership, LLC, corporation	Member ownership, cooperative	Multi-stakeholder cooperative
Governance	Board of directors, hierarchical management, one-dollar, one-vote	Board of directors, assembly, one-member, one-vote	Multi-stakeholder governance, one-member, one-vote, sociocracy, heterarchy, consensus, holacracy
Capital access, revenue model	Private investments, stock markets, venture capital, loans, earnings	Membership, credit union loans, retained earnings	Grants, donations, crowdfunding, market mechanisms (sales, fees, subscriptions)
Objective	Shareholder value, profit maximization, growth	Sustainability, equitable distribution of resources, the well-being of members or the community, fair pay, and pricing	Sustainability, equitable distribution of resources, the well-being of members or the community, fair pay, and pricing
Property rights, R&D, innovation	Intellectual property (IP), patents, trademarks, and copyrights, centralized R&D, rent extraction, planned obsolescence	Protected IP, closed proprietary licenses, not producing commons	Open protocols, open supply chains, commons, many-to-many innovation, circular economy, modularity, repairability, adaptability, maintenance
Labor management	Division of labour, salaries, value extraction	Division of labour, salaries, value distribution	Do-ocracy, stigmergy, salaries, value distribution, contributory accounting

Chapter 3

ENVISIONING THE POST-HEGEMONY OF OPEN COOPERATIVISM

This book adheres to the reformist strand in the literature of the commons without excluding convergences with liberal and anti-capitalist trajectories towards a commons-based post-capitalist transition. As such, the book explores the potential merge of the digital commons and cosmolocalism with platform cooperatives on the model of open cooperativism. The book builds on the work of scholars who aim to extend Ostrom's design principles from natural commons to urban and digital commons, as well as the broader cooperative economy (De Filippi et al. 2024; Foster and Iaione 2019; Guttmann 2021; Rozas et al. 2021). It aims to bridge Ostrom's design principles with traditional cooperative principles in the model of open cooperativism (Figure 3.1).

To address the challenges identified in the previous section, this book proposes integrating Ostrom's eighth design principle of nested enterprises with the cooperative movement's sixth principle of intercooperation.

Ostrom's design principles	Traditional/ platform cooperatives	Open cooperative	POSTCAPITALISM Key performance indicators	Conventional value chain
Boundaries Locality	Voluntary open membership Member economic participation	Common-pool resources: natural resources infrastructures information knowledge skills capital	Economic sustainability: cost-efficiency ratio total factor productivity equity distribution reinvestment rate	Firm infrastructure HR management Sales
Self-management Monitoring Sanctioning Conflict-resolution	Democracy Education	Commoning: stigmergy modularity open protocols open supply chains open logistics circular economy contributory accounting	Environmental sustainability: carbon footprint resource use innovation rate supply chain efficiency production/consumption index Digital Product Passport	Technology Product planning Manufacturing Logistics
Autonomy Nested Enterprises	Autonomy Cooperation Community	Community: multistakeholder cooperative (ethical market entities, civil society, partner state)	Social sustainability: member engagement gender ratio local impact network effects human rights	Communication Marketing Service

Figure 3.1. Merging the Commons with Cooperatives

This approach leverages the concept of the commons as a strategic framework to facilitate stronger intercooperation among ethical market entities, specifically cooperatives and civil society organizations, through a model of open cooperativism.

The book employs the model of open cooperativism as a floating signifier (Laclau and Mouffe 2001) attached to hybrid organizational forms such as cooperatives, civil society organizations, ethical market entities, social enterprises, small and medium enterprises, foundations, institutions, makerspaces, fablabs and municipalities. The empty signifier of open cooperativism floats around three nodal points—the digital commons, cooperativism and user communities—that recombine with various other elements such as democracy, value distribution, and sustainability in different degrees and organizational settings. The book does not restrict the use of the term "cooperativism" to the cooperative sector alone but it loosely applies the term to denote collaboration between diverse organizational forms and legal entities that fall under the banner of "open cooperativism."

Kostakis and Bauwens (2014) advocate for the merge of civil society organizations—foundations, not-for-profits, institutions, the social and solidarity economy—and ethical market entities—cooperatives, social enterprises, SMEs, and for-benefit corporations—under commons-based peer production to effectively challenge extractive capitalism and embrace regenerative post-capitalism (Figure 3.2). Ethical market entities that engage in co-producing or accessing commons through reciprocity gain a competitive advantage over closed, proprietary models like platform capitalism. By

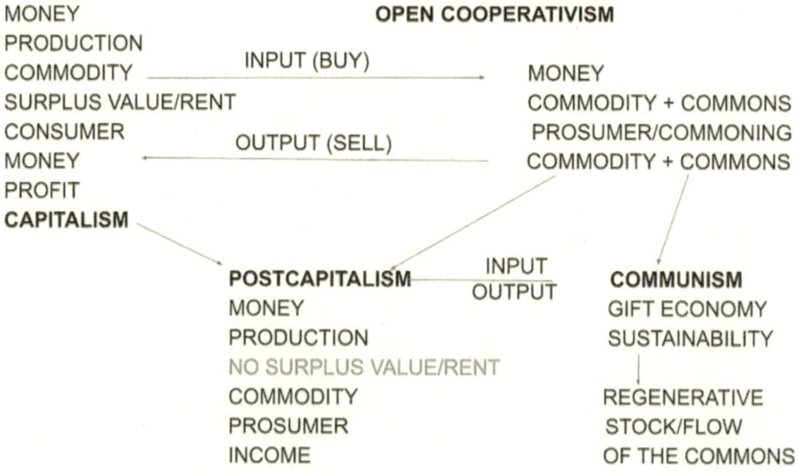

Figure 3.2. Toward post-capitalism

tapping into common-pool resources through co-production or fee-based access, these entities benefit from knowledge diffusion, innovation spillovers, and reduced production and transaction costs. This enables them to create scarcity for the market while generating abundance for civil society.

In collaboration with an enabling state, ethical market entities and civil society organizations can form a multi-stakeholder interface for open cooperativism. This approach facilitates the coproduction of common goods, meets social needs, promotes bottom-up innovation, fosters sustainability, enhances resilience, and supports a circular (gift) economy alongside a postcapitalist market. In essence, open cooperativism introduces an asymmetric form of *coopetition* with platform capitalism, built on joint development and shared ownership models. By pooling resources and developing shared solutions, open cooperatives aim to establish a commons-based, ethical, and sustainable postcapitalist economy.

However, employing the commons as a factor of production in a cooperative economy is a double-edged sword that may exacerbate the structural weaknesses and tensions inherent in traditional and platform co-ops. While this model has the potential to address market inefficiencies in the reproduction of common goods, it struggles with corporate co-optation and the lack of sustainable business models that can both regenerate the commons and provide livelihoods for the user communities that produce them. Despite encapsulating both social and environmental sustainability, commons-based peer production remains structurally incapable of sustaining itself (Bauwens and Pantazis, 2018). One of its core challenges is the difficulty of establishing functional institutions that enable communities to capture value and ensure stable income for contributors. Additionally, enforcement mechanisms for securing contributions in digital and global commons remain ambiguous, and it is unclear whether network effects and innovation spillovers are sufficient to offset efficiency losses.

Transitional and prefigurative institutions supporting this model emerge through continuous experimentation, often operating in hybrid or "grey" zones. However, these experimental models have yet to be tested at scale in competitive markets. Commons-based peer production coexists with capitalist economies that rely on closed intellectual property, venture capital, and for-profit corporate structures, making it subordinate to hyper-competitive market dynamics. The long-term sustainability and viability of these hybrid approaches remain uncertain.

Digital commons face unique challenges, including managing collective investments, ensuring fair revenue distribution, addressing organizational issues such as turnover and trust, navigating legal ambiguities, protecting brand identity, establishing reputation systems, and developing sound business strategies. While commons-based peer production holds distinct advantages over investor-owned firms, its openness makes it difficult to establish a self-sustaining business model. Ultimately, the extent to which it can provide stable livelihoods or support viable enterprises remains an open question.

To address the challenges of the commons and the cooperative economy, the book introduces a political theory and economic framework that balances the profit motive and individual interest with mutualism and collective well-being. It puts forth a moral and economic restructuring of market incentives around a commons-based mode of production self-governed by diverse stakeholders, transcending national, religious, class, sexual, cultural, and ideological boundaries. It merges the commons with traditional and platform cooperatives under the model of open cooperativism. This model, rooted in economic democracy, is anchored on shared, collectively designed incentives that ensure the equitable and sustainable distribution and governance of common-pool resources according to the principle: from each according to their capacities, to each according to their needs. Thus, the model of open cooperativism brings together the social and solidarity economy with social entrepreneurship under a postcapitalist economic democracy that identifies the common good with the commons.

The book champions a postcapitalist vision of economic democracy, advocating for the "commoning" of the common good—a radical democratization of both state politics and market economies geared toward the model of open cooperativism. Open cooperativism operates on business models that produce common-pool resources, which serve as focal points of cooperation for multiple stakeholders. The core argument centers on reconstructing the incentive structure of market economies, moving toward a political theory of the common good as a commons that reconciles liberal and Marxist values such as freedom, equality, pluralism, overlapping consensus, and mutualism, within an open cooperativist model.

Right-wing neoliberal populism decouples democracy from the economy, emphasizing neo-conservative morals, protectionism, autocratic nationalism, profit motives, and individual interests. In contrast, left-wing populism reinforces a statist approach to hegemony that fails to integrate pluralism into its vision of the common good. Ernesto Laclau and Chantal Mouffe (2001) seek to dissociate from the economism and classism of traditional Marxism and reinvigorate hegemony from the standpoint of articulating a chain of equivalence across diverse demands such as the ones of feminism, ecology, and market socialism, to mention a few. But still they cannot but reproduce the hegelo-marxian dialectics that they seek to avoid inasmuch as they divide the social and political space into two opposing blocks, that is, two antagonistic chains of equivalence. In Laclau and Mouffe's framework, dualism revolves around two antagonistic chains of equivalence that are constantly engaged in negating one another with the aim of occupying state politics in terms of hegemony.

The division of *the social* into two antagonistic blocks is an oversimplification that does not follow either ontologically or analytically. The very ontological principles of conflict, antagonism, and difference they philosophically endorse do not necessarily unfold in two opposing camps of meaning. Heterogeneity and difference allow for multiple interpretations of meaning and social imaginaries. Conflict is not the sole mode of doing politics. By prioritizing conflict over consensus, Laclau and Mouffe run counter to the radical pluralism they put forth. They, thus, remain trapped into an old-school leftism that limits the postcapitalist socioeconomic alternatives they seem to espouse.

In short, Laclau and Mouffe reproduce an ontological and normative dualism of simplistic conceptualizations such as necessity and contingency, articulation, and dislocation, *politics* and *the political*, the particular and the universal, openness and enclosure of meaning, identity and difference. As an ontological cause and effect, conflict is the overarching modus vivendi of politics. Yet, the reversed dialectics of Laclau and Mouffe's hegemony is a misrepresentation and distortion of the inherent pluralism of *the social*. Rather than advancing freedom and equality in favor of pluralism, conflict alone limits the potential of radical democracy. Democracy is not set solely against the backdrop of conflict but can take different forms, meanings, and dynamics such as consensus, mutualism, and win–win partnerships.

While right-wing neoliberal populism remains the dominant hegemonic discourse, left-wing populism lacks a compelling narrative capable of mobilizing a critical mass to establish a counter-hegemony. This shortfall underscores the absence of a political framework capable of nudging the libertarian ethos underpinning neoliberal populism towards a more inclusive, ethical, and sustainable economy. To put it simply, most people today do not vote for the Left, with some of them being even anti-Leftist.

The retreat of the Left is not primarily due to its disconnection with the working class. Rather, it stems from the absence of a coherent political narrative, strategy, and plan capable of articulating a chain of equivalence around a mutually beneficial mode of production that addresses the interests of all people. It is neither an issue of the periodic crises of capitalism and the presumed inevitable democratic ascent of socialism and communism. Nor of antagonistic blocs that compete to hegemonize state politics. Instead, the failure of the Left lies in the lack of a viable postcapitalist alternative capable of reaching a critical mass. The ideal of communism ought to embrace all people irrespective of class and not exclude people by means of the hegemony of one alliance of people over the others.

The fragmentation of the Left mirrors the fragmentation of the social and solidarity economy, as well as the cooperative movement as a whole. This reflects tensions between radicalism and social democracy, between the social and solidarity economy and social entrepreneurship, between a gift economy and market economies, and between the commons and commercialization. It also highlights the dichotomy between use value and exchange value. Opposition, contradictions, tensions and fragmentation become all the more problematic since cooperatives have been associated with left-leaning or anti-business ideologies. Historically, co-ops were considered enterprises for the "have-nots" and maintained a strong connection with the worker movement (Battilani and Schröter, 2012). During the years co-ops developed an ideological flexibility encompassing various movements, from the working class to the religious minded, from liberal to anti-corporation-oriented movements. However, still today, the movement is perceived by many as a defensive reaction, a means of protecting certain groups, such as labor, from the harshest aspects of capitalistic change.

Co-ops along with nongovernmental associations are most often grouped together under the social economy or civic economy that encompasses a diverse variety of organizations: public-private partnerships, socially responsible companies, community enterprises, cooperatives, foundations, charities, voluntary bodies, ethical investment funds, credit unions, community, banks, the informal sector (the ethical part), and nongovernment organizations. These organizations aim to serve the interests of all stakeholders involved: customers, the local community, the organization's staff, and the providers of capital. Yet, the identification of the cooperative movement with the social economy or the third or fourth sector of the economy is detrimental to the transformative potential of a postcapitalist economy.

In essence, populism reflects a deeper moral crisis, owing to the lack of a normative political theory that can reconnect democracy and economics under a sustainable mode of production, which would be mutually beneficial for multiple stakeholders. It is not the place here to set the stage for a normative political theory capable of establishing post-capitalism. Rather, the goal is to allude to some basic normative principles of reconfiguring politics and the economy towards a radical democratic pluralism. This new vision, framed as "open cooperativism," would bring together civil society organizations, ethical market entities, and a "partner state" as stakeholders in a collaborative model of governance. The politics of open cooperativism endorses neither an ideal speech situation aiming for consensus on the force of the better argument (Habermas 1996) nor a conflictual consensus that seeks to constantly reinvigorate antagonism between counter-hegemonic blocks (Mouffe 2000, 2005). Rather, it encompasses consensus and conflict on a case-by-case basis driven by an overlapping consensus (Rawls 1971) over core substantial values that underpin the common sense of society such as freedom, equality, difference, pluralism, mutualism, and sustainability. The political restructuring of incentives around the core principles of a post-capitalist economic democracy would develop along the lines of a partner state enabling sustainable business models of open cooperativism.

The role of the partner state (Pazaitis and Drechsler 2021) is crucial in that direction since it dissociates from a distributionist, neoliberal, socialist, or mission-oriented state by integrating commons-based peer production across rural, urban, local, municipal, national, international and cosmolocal settings. Representative democracy would be extended through participatory mechanisms (participatory legislation, participatory budgeting, online and offline deliberation mechanisms, liquid voting, real-time democratic consultations and procedures, proxy voting mechanisms). The state should be de-bureaucratized through the decentralization of public services via public-commons partnerships. Traditional and bureaucratic hierarchies should be transformed or replaced by poly-governance models of participation and deliberation that include user communities and other stakeholders (Bauwens et al. 2019).

A partner state (Figure 3.3) should devise policies to support participatory governance and participatory budgeting of state-funded technological education, state-funded technologies of public utility and interest such as open-source libraries, makerspaces, FabLabs, and technological parks hosting public-commons partnerships among multiple stakeholders such as municipalities, civil society organizations, ethical market entities, freelancers, digital nomads, etc.

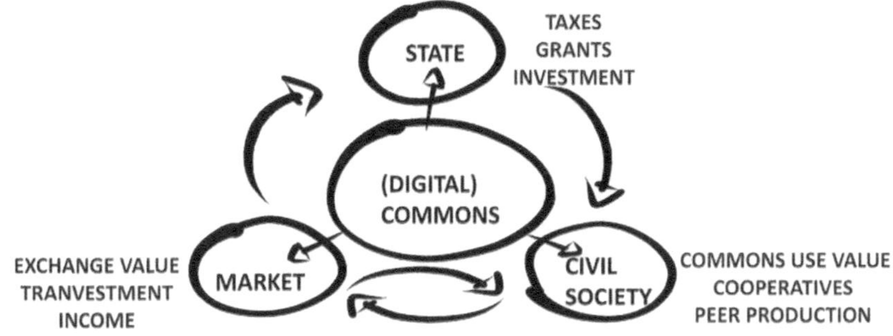

Figure 3.3. A Partner State

Thus, a partner state would make use of open-source technologies to gain on efficiency, agility, and adaptability, save on public expenditures, reduce trade deficits, boost innovation and collaboration, equitably distribute value among multiple stakeholders, foster sustainability and circular economies, enhance democracy, reclaim technological sovereignty and autonomy, and promote open-source business models to transform sectors of the economy toward a fairer and freer society.

The ultimate goal would be to reimagine politics in the model of open cooperativism between the commons, ethical market entities and a partner state, setting out to establish the counter-hegemony of a commons-based post-capitalist transition vis-à-vis the current hegemony of neoliberalism.

The model of open cooperativism still rests on thin conceptual and empirical foundations. The current book seeks to shed some light on commons-based peer production by presenting key findings from a three-year research project on Internet-enabled grassroots organizational models, including platform cooperatives, the digital commons, cosmo-localism, and open cooperatives. This book illustrates some empirical instances of open cooperativism to help envision the counter-hegemony of a commons-based post-capitalist ethical and sustainable economy and politics. Adopting a conceptually driven and empirically grounded approach, it explores both the potential and the challenges of commons-based peer production. Ultimately, the study examines the normative and empirical conditions shaping platform and open cooperatives, aiming to generate valuable insights for both researchers and practitioners, including theoretical and practical implications for future research.

Chapter 4

METHODOLOGY

The book draws on empirical research conducted for the purposes of a three-year research project entitled "Techno-Social Innovation in the Collaborative Economy". Empirical research adopts a case study approach (Yin 2014), particularly suitable for exploring innovative organizational models such as digital commons, cosmolocalism, platform cooperativism, and open cooperativism. The selection criteria for the case studies include:

- Alignment with the design principles of commons-based peer production.
- Creation of multidimensional value across diverse economic sectors (e.g., agriculture, food distribution, bike delivery, finance).
- Participation within broader cosmolocal economic ecosystems, offering ample contexts for open cooperativism.
- Allowance for cross-national and cross-regional empirical analysis of social innovation practices within commons-based peer production.

The book builds upon empirical findings previously documented in standalone case-study papers (Papadimitropoulos 2023; Papadimitropoulos and Malamidis 2023; Papadimitropoulos and Malamidis 2023; Papadimitropoulos and Perperidis 2024). Data collection methods include desktop research, literature review, participatory observation, and semi-structured, in-depth interviews (Fiss, 2009) with key stakeholders. The book author and principal investigator actively participated in workshops, online meetings, and general assemblies. In total, 34 members from P2P Lab, Tzoumakers, Open Food Network, CoopCycle, and Circles UBI were interviewed, with interview durations ranging from 40 to 100 minutes. Interviews were recorded via Skype and transcribed using Descript software. The case studies of Subvert and Transkribus are also added, which are based on recent research conducted beyond the scope of the three-year research project titled "*Techno-Social Innovation in the Collaborative Economy.*" The methodology used to examine these case studies involves literature review and desktop research.

Data analysis followed an inductive qualitative coding strategy inspired by grounded theory methods (Fiss 2009), combined with theory-informed analytical categories derived from the literature on open cooperativism. The analytical process unfolded in three sequential stages. In the first stage, open coding, interview transcripts and field notes were coded inductively to identify recurrent discourses/practices. This phase produced a wide range of descriptive first-order codes closely grounded in participants' own language and everyday experiences.

In the second stage, axial coding, these first-order codes were systematically clustered into four second-order analytical dimensions common across all cases: Value Proposition (how each initiative defines its social, economic, and environmental purpose), Governance (how power, participation, and coordination are organized), Economic Model (revenue streams, redistribution mechanisms, labor compensation, and sustainability strategies), and Law/Policy (legal status, licensing regimes, regulatory constraints, and relations with public-sector actors). These four dimensions formed the core comparative framework guiding the empirical analysis.

The third stage consisted of a cross-case thematic synthesis, in which findings were compared across the four cases to identify recurrent patterns, structural contradictions, enabling institutional conditions, and constraints on scalability and long-term sustainability. Analytical rigor and internal validity were strengthened through data triangulation across interviews, documentary sources, and participant observation (Gibbert et al. 2008); systematic crosscase comparison to test the robustness of emerging interpretations; and iterative movement between empirical material and the theoretical framework of open cooperativism. This multilayered approach ensured that the analytical claims were both empirically grounded and theoretically informed.

This research differentiates itself from existing literature (Avanzo et al., 2023; Borrits, 2019a, 2019b; Pantazis and Meyer, 2020; Wallace 2026) by analyzing empirical data explicitly through the lens of open cooperativism. It particularly emphasizes the theoretical and practical implications for long-term structural change through establishing a counter-hegemony to prevailing platform capitalism. The crosscase analysis conducted in this study significantly enriches the existing fragmented scholarly discussions by enabling cross-sectoral insights, comparative analysis, and generalized conclusions regarding the transformative potential of platform and open cooperative models.

Chapter 5

CASE STUDIES

5.1. Tzoumakers

Tzoumakers[1] (Figure 5.1) is a pilot project incubated by the P2P Lab,[2] a research collective situated at Ioannina, Greece. P2P Lab participates in state-funded research programs (EU grants), carrying out research on grassroots organizational models such as cosmolocalism and commons-based peer production. The Tzoumakers project was initiated initially as part of the Phygital project funded by the Interreg research program.[3] Later, P2P Lab received funding from the European Research Council (ERC) to launch Tzoumakers as the Greek pilot of the cosmolocalism project.[4]

Tzoumakers is a community of farmers, peasants, researchers, and social entrepreneurs experimenting with open-source agriculture (Giotitsas 2019) (Table 5.1). The initiative aims to address the lack of commercially available agricultural tools for small-scale farming in mountainous regions, as well as the hegemony of closed, costly agricultural technologies that are unaffordable and non-repairable for smallholder farmers (Pantazis and Meyer, 2020). To this end, P2P Lab, in collaboration with the municipality of Ioannina and the local community of farmers and entrepreneurs (Tzoumakers) located in the Tzoumerka mountain region, established a makerspace in the village of Kalentzi, near the city of Ioannina. The makerspace is equipped with computer numerical control (CNC) machinery, including a welding station, a laser cutter, a milling machine, and sensors, which are used, among other purposes, for the manufacturing of small-scale open-source agricultural tools (Pantazis and Meyer, 2020). The municipality of Ioannina pays for electricity and bills.

1 https://www.tzoumakers.gr/english/
2 https://p2plab.org/
3 https://ec.europa.eu/regional_policy/en/projects/Cyprus/phygital-community-workshops-in-balkan-med-countries-deliver-smart-open-access-solutions-thanks-to-interreg
4 https://www.cosmolocalism.eu/

Figure 5.1. Tzoumakers

Table 5.1. Discourses in P2P Lab/Tzoumakers

Value proposition	Governance	Economy	Law
The digital commons, cosmolocalism, open-source agriculture, technological sovereignty, circular economy, degrowth **Problem**: the absence of commercial agricultural tools for small-scale agriculture **Solution**: peer production of on-demand customisable low-cost tools	Direct democracy, decentralization, multi-stakeholder governance, heterarchy **Multiple stakeholders**: core members, fellow researchers, affiliates, third-party community members, farmers, community members, the municipality **Workshops**: open participation calls	**Revenue streams**: EU grants, donations, crowdfunding	Non-profit organization, EU, municipality **Licenses**: copyleft, Creative Commons

Inspired by initiatives such as FarmHack[5] and L'Atelier Paysan,[6] Tzoumakers organize participatory workshops in which agricultural tools are co-designed and manufactured on demand. Participation is initiated through open calls disseminated via social media and the Tzoumakers website, inviting

5 https://farmhack.org/tools

6 https://www.latelierpaysan.org/

interested actors to submit proposals for the development of demand-driven, customizable tools addressing local needs. Once a workshop is scheduled, a coordinator—either a member of P2P Lab or a local technician—is appointed to oversee the manufacturing process. The tools are co-designed through a democratic process involving all participants. For instance, a stainless-steel aromatic herb grinder was developed in response to requests from farmers based in the island of Crete, who were unwilling to pay the approximately €12,000 required to purchase a comparable commercial grinder. To date, Tzoumakers has organized 30 workshops and developed 13 different types of agricultural tools, including a legume-harvesting machine, a fencing-post hammer, a tilling fork, and an aromatic herb grinder. All blueprints, bills of materials, and assembly instructions are openly shared on the project's website. Thus, the makerspace, machinery, designs, and tools collectively constitute both material and immaterial commons, freely accessible and reusable on demand.

Following the conclusion of the funding period provided by P2P Lab, Tzoumakers convened a general assembly to develop a business model that would determine the project's continuity and the long-term sustainability of the makerspace. Since 2023, the School of Earth[7] (also known as Nea Guinea) has assumed the role of coordinator of the Tzoumakers makerspace in Kalentzi. In recent years, the makerspace has gradually shifted away from its original focus on the manufacturing of agricultural tools and has primarily functioned as an open-source toolkit library, utilized by a wide range of local actors for diverse purposes. For example, the School of Earth has used the space to manufacture and repair wind turbines; the local mountaineering club to construct posts and signage; local entrepreneurs to produce boards, benches, and other items; and artisans to carry out various small-scale constructions and repairs.

In addition to its emphasis on practical tool-making, the Tzoumakers initiative functions as a living laboratory for exploring alternative economic models that transcend traditional capitalist structures. The project highlights how cosmolocalism can occupy economic niches unaddressed by corporate interests, particularly in small-scale, mountainous agriculture where market incentives are absent. The strategic location of the fab lab in Tzoumerka, combined with its active collaboration with local farmers and cooperatives, fosters a regenerative approach to both economy and community. By offering open-source designs and on-demand production, the project not only reduces costs but also democratizes technological access, positioning the community as co-creators rather than passive consumers. This participatory process

7 https://neaguinea.org/en/s

builds trust, enhances local resilience, and creates a platform for innovation in sectors where conventional solutions fall short.

The Tzoumakers initiative has evolved into a distinctive model of open cooperativism, incorporating Ostrom's principle of nested enterprises alongside the cooperative principle of intercooperation. It operates as a community-driven, multidimensional project integrating diverse stakeholders, including commons-producing actors (farmers, technicians, researchers), ethical market entities (social enterprises and local cooperatives), and institutional partners such as the European Research Council (ERC) and the municipality of Ioannina, providing critical financial and infrastructural support.

Specifically, Tzoumakers embodies three key dimensions of open cooperativism:

- Commons production: A community of farmers, researchers, technicians, and citizens collaboratively design and manufacture agricultural tools and artifacts.
- Ethical economic engagement: Social enterprises and local cooperatives actively participate in workshops, contributing to the co-creation of socially and environmentally beneficial products.
- Institutional support: External institutions, notably the ERC and local municipal authorities, supply essential resources, including funding and infrastructure, enhancing the project's sustainability and scalability.

Despite its accomplishments, Tzoumakers face a number of challenges, including the lack of substantial institutional support that would create incentives for young farmers to turn to open agriculture, the absence of appropriate licensing frameworks for open hardware, as well as the municipality's plans to convert the makerspace into a guesthouse as part of a broader process of rural touristification and gentrification. The lack of a clear legal framework for open-source hardware and open cooperatives hampers scalability and legal protection. Additionally, the project contends with limited farmer participation due to unfamiliarity with digital technologies and skepticism toward publicly funded initiatives. To address these challenges, the community seeks to secure funding in order to employ two salaried staff members for the next 18 months to operate the makerspace on a daily basis. In the longer term, there are ideas to branch out the makerspace in the city of Ioannina and operate it as a repair café serving entrepreneurs and small- and medium-sized enterprises.

These challenges underscore the need for institutional innovation, such as the development of dedicated open hardware licensing schemes and supportive policy frameworks. Furthermore, sustained scaling would benefit from stronger integration with ethical market entities and partner-state structures that can anchor Tzoumakers in stable economic and governance models, ensuring long-term viability and amplifying its counter-hegemonic potential. Addressing these issues requires sustained intercooperation, robust institutional partnerships, and continued engagement with local communities to maintain its commitment to regenerative and inclusive economic practices.

5.2. Open Food Network

The Open Food Network[8] (OFN) was launched in 2012 by two farmers from Violet Town in Australia in response to the growing disconnection between producers and consumers resulting from food supply chain centralization driven by market concentration (Ortolan 2020). Middlemen, corporations, and big supermarkets were squeezing out income from farmers while at the same time undermining food quality, producing food waste, threatening biodiversity, and exacerbating climate change.

The OFN has evolved during the years into an open-sourced e-commerce platform that aligns farmers, user communities and ethical market entities around the launch of short food supply chains (SFSCs) across the globe (OFN Handbook, n.d.). SFSCs cut out the middlemen by directly interconnecting producers and consumers (Figure 5.2). They come to address, among others, the profit squeeze most prevalent in agriculture, with farmers getting paid the 1% of their produce sold in the market (Table 5.2). The remaining 99% is variously allocated to taxes, production costs, processors, suppliers, wholesalers and retailers. In doing so, SFSCs address key social and economic issues by ensuring higher income for producers, promoting sustainable and ecologically responsible agricultural practices, providing fresh and high-quality food to consumers, and revitalizing local economies and communities (Jarzębowski et al. 2020: p.2). "The result is customers are getting better, fresher, more ethically raised food. In return, farmers get direct lines of feedback from their customers, less food waste and more money in their pockets" (Cornish 2019).

The OFN platform is run by a global community of volunteers and members. It now hosts more than 7000 producers in over 20 countries around the world. The back-end of the platform open sources the code behind the front-end that features a directory, a map, shop fronts and logistics such as products listing, products stock, orders, etc. Democratic participation is a key feature of the OFN operating around five Circles: (1) Delivery (code, software); (2) Marketing/Communications; (3) Governance; (4) Fundraising;

8 https://openfoodnetwork.org.au/

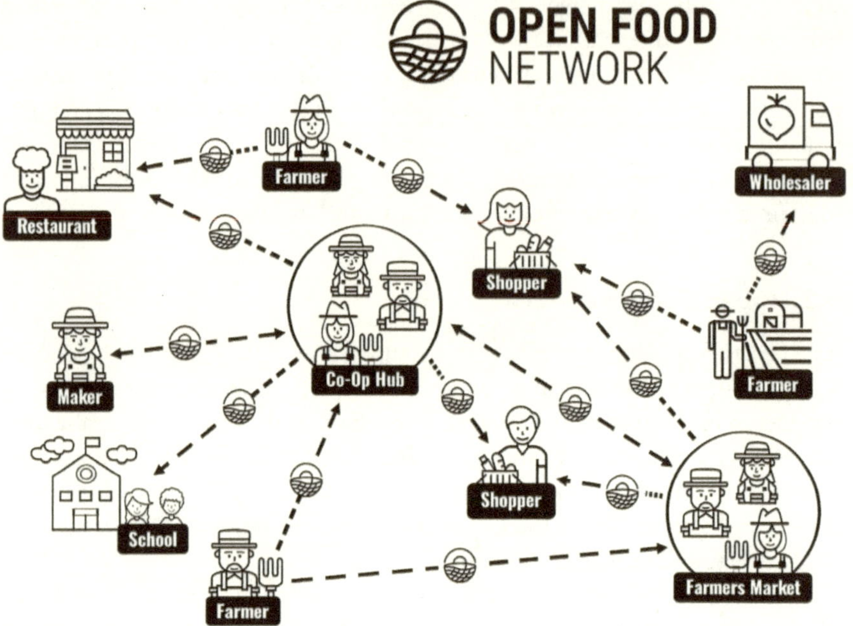

Figure 5.2. Open Food Network

and (5) Other Services/Providers. Circles are coordinated by representatives of the network's five core instances (OFN Australia, OFN France, OFN UK, OFN Canada and OFN USA).

Decision-making is based on the principles of subsidiarity and sociocracy. Subsidiarity distributes authority locally. It secures operational autonomy for local instances, thereby allowing for decentralization, relocalization, and resilience. Sociocracy draws on the use of consent rather than majority voting. If no objection is raised, decision-making settles around a lazy consensus, otherwise a decision is reached by the 2/3 majority voting. These principles foster resilience and flexibility but also introduce tensions between volunteer and paid contributions, and between grassroots experimentation and the need for standardized structures. The model's granularity and do-ocratic approach allow community members to self-assign tasks, but also risk creating informal hierarchies and inefficiencies if volunteer commitment varies. Global community meetings are taking place on a monthly basis online.

The OFN software reduces the role of intermediaries and lowers administrative and transaction costs, thereby contributing to fair pay for

Table 5.2. Discourses in Open Food Network

Value proposition	Governance	Economy	Law
The digital commons, SFSCs, agroecology, systemic change, food sovereignty **Problem**: food centralization and disconnection, profit squeeze **Solution**: decentralization and inter-connection via SFSCs **Economic sustainability**: fair pay, lower costs, reduced information asymmetry, consumer empowerment, producer-consumer reconnection **Social sustainability**: inclusion, relocalisation, reduced health inequality and food poverty, community building **Environmental sustainability**: recycling waste, organic, permaculture, reduction in CO2 emissions, resource efficiency, biodiversity	Multi-stakeholder governance **OFN Global**: five coordination Circles **Decision-making**: subsidiarity, sociocracy, lazy consensus **Stakeholders**: farmers/ growers, food processors, food hubs, shoppers, distributors, consumers, associates (white label users), service providers, volunteers	**Revenue streams**: fundraising, grants, subscriptions, fees, OFN instances contribution, crowdfunding, partnerships **Fair pay for farmers**: cutting out the middlemen > decrease of production and transaction costs **Fair pay for OFN employees**: payment according to the cost-of-living index by country (10–40 euro per hour) **fair pay for OFN employees**: payment according to the cost-of-living index by country (10–40 euro per hour) **Business models**: producers selling directly to customers or indirectly through food coops, farmers' markets and food hubs **Transparency**: open budget spreadsheet	**For-benefit foundation**: the Open Food Foundation **Community pledge**: informal legal agreement food certification: compliance with organic and food safety standards **Food certification**: compliance with organic and food safety standards **Open-source content and code**: licensed with CC BY-SA 3.0 and AGPL 3 respectively Data food **interoperability**: common standards and protocols **Community food enterprises**: not-for-profits, charities, associations, local food markets, coops, social enterprises, community interest enterprises, community supported agriculture

farmers and food hubs participating in the platform. To achieve this, the network applies a two-tier economic model: on the one hand, resources are allocated to support the development and maintenance of the shared software (e.g., wages for developers, testers); on the other hand, resources are used to provide services to users (OFN Handbook, n.d.). These costs are primarily covered through fundraising and grants, with local OFN instances contributing either 40% of their revenue (generated through subscriptions and fees) or 40% of their time to support global activities. The OFN is legally backed by the Open Food Foundation, which is a not-for-profit entity overseen by a board operating in Australia. The Open Food Foundation aims to protect the OFN digital commons of software and code, which are licensed under CC BY-SA 3.0. and AGPL3, respectively. The OFN is currently in the process of implementing data food interoperability across the different platforms interconnected through the OFN. Data food interoperability "will enable a data standard so that multiple different platforms, including the Open Food Network and other open-source platforms and several proprietary platforms will work together so that farmers and growers and food producers can list their products on one of those platforms, and their data would be available to other platforms" (Interviewee).

Overall, the Open Food Network advocates for systemic change in agriculture by promoting agroecological practices and democratically governed, community-based food enterprises. Yet, systemic change is in tension with institutional and operational diversity across the OFN ecosystem, which often breeds fragmentation and contradictions. One interviewee highlighted such challenges: "There's tension between not-for-profit, open-source philosophy and closed-source profit-making; individual gain versus collective gain." OFN's emphasis on practical aspects like business management and data interoperability sometimes overshadows broader societal goals.

The OFN's economic model emphasizes fairness and transparency, striving to reduce profit extraction by intermediaries. By offering producers diverse business models—from direct sales to cooperation with food hubs and co-ops—the platform allows for local adaptability. However, the platform's financial sustainability heavily depends on grants, fundraising, and volunteer contributions, which raises questions about long-term stability and potential vulnerability to market fluctuations. The emphasis on open-source principles also brings challenges in terms of potential corporate co-optation, requiring robust licensing (e.g., copyfair licensing) and constant vigilance to protect the commons from being appropriated by closed-source profit-driven entities. Therefore, while OFN contributes significantly toward business efficiency, sustainability, and practical solutions, its potential for fostering radical systemic change may face limitations inherent to navigating between short-term pragmatism and long-term transformative objectives.

5.3. CoopCycle

CoopCycle[9] is an informal federation encompassing over 67 bike delivery cooperatives operating globally (Spier 2022). Formally established as a France-based association, CoopCycle is led by volunteers who create and manage open-source software designed specifically for bike delivery cooperatives (Figure 5.3). This association provides critical digital infrastructure and organizational support, empowering a worldwide network of bike delivery cooperatives.

Originally founded as a response to the precarious working conditions faced by couriers within the gig economy, CoopCycle emerged from efforts to replicate and transform proprietary food delivery software into a digital commons, released under a Coopyleft license[10] This licensing framework restricts use of the software to cooperatives and collectives that comply with the principles of the social and solidarity economy, thereby preventing its appropriation by profit-driven platform corporations while enabling collective ownership, democratic governance, and worker empowerment (Table 5.3).

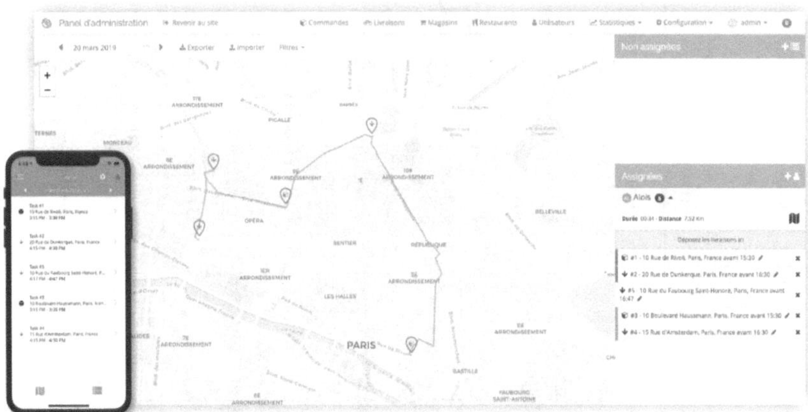

Figure 5.3. CoopCycle

9 https://coopcycle.org/
10 https://coopcycle.org/coopyleft/

Table 5.3. Discourses in CoopCycle

Value proposition	Governance	Economy	Law
Problem: foodtech platform precarization and uberization **Solution**: the digital provision of bike-delivery e-logistics and services **Services**: software development; onboarding and training; food delivery; last mile **Economic sustainability**: cost reduction; fair pay; the sharing of value **Social sustainability**: local and ethical social economy; solidarity; care **Environmental sustainability**: less traffic and noise; reduced waste and CO_2 emission	**Federation**: 67 co-ops across 10 countries; three employees (two developers, one coordinator); a board of eight administrators; working groups **Decision-making**: general annual assembly; monthly co-op assembly; one coop, one vote; one member, one vote; consent-based decision; majority voting; sociocracy **Centralization**: hard and heavy software development (back-end) **Decentralization**: software customization; co-op self-management; marketing, pricing strategy	**Federation revenue streams**: 2,5% of the added value of co-ops annual turnover (500 euros minimum annual fee); donations; grants; awards; consulting services **Co-op revenue streams**: delivery fee 20–30% **Fair pay**: replace volunteer work in the federation with paid work; couriers paid by the hour; annual profits distributed to workers **Partnerships**: MAIF; MACIF (insurance); FACTTIC Argentina; ITDP Mexico:	Multi-stakeholder cooperative; worker-owned cooperatives; non-profit social inclusion companies; Coopyleft license **Legal entity**: formally a French association, informally a federation, a precursor to a multi-stakeholder cooperative Coopyleft license **Partnership agreement**: associations and collectives joining the federation commit to becoming a cooperative within 2 years

CoopCycle caters for "the creation of an anti-capitalist economic model based on the Commons, the development of the CoopCycle software (UI/UX, dev, trainings, docs, aso.), political lobbying, juridical toolbox, global coordination" (CoopCycle n.d.b). To this end, and unlike traditional and platform cooperatives that have trouble in scaling, CoopCycle has managed to scale globally as a federation. Early on from its outset, CoopCycle went international, with cooperatives from France, Belgium, Germany, and Spain becoming members of the federation (Democracy at Work 2021). The launch of CoopCycle Latinoamérica in 2021 (Kasparian 2022) as well as the links with NGOs, trade unions, financial institutions, local authorities, and other actors of the social and solidarity economy, are significant milestones along the roadmap to establishing an anti-capitalist block.

Unlike traditional foodtech platforms, which treat workers as independent contractors and pay per delivery, CoopCycle compensates workers on an hourly basis, providing them secure employment benefits including social security, insurance, paid sick leave, and holiday entitlements. Rather than prioritizing shareholder profits, CoopCycle focuses on equitable value distribution among workers, encapsulated in the dictum: "Money should not make money. All benefits should go to workers. You need to ride a bike to earn money" (Riders Collective, 2021).

However, the competition is unfair: thanks to freelancing and fundraising money, profit-driven platforms can afford to charge extremely low prices with the only objective of completely killing the competition. They can afford to hire more workers and capture a larger share of the market. Contrary to profit-driven platforms, platform co-ops bear additional costs since they pay taxes and workers' benefits such as social security, insurance, sick day and holiday leave pay. One should also add inflationary pressures where demand for fast delivery services is slowing amid the cost-of-living crisis.

To adjust, CoopCycle expands operations on last-mile delivery since many cities outsource to bike delivery co-ops for environmental reasons (Interviewee). CoopCycle can thus take advantage of decentralized networks in local commerce and attract new clients and member co-ops. CoopCycle can also sell decarbonating services to municipalities. CoopCycle, finally, intends to standardize prices for big clients, put forward a business plan as a central filter, and develop a media strategy.

By choosing bicycles for delivery, CoopCycle actively leads in reducing the food delivery sector's carbon footprint. Its environmental commitment is central to its value proposition, forming strategic partnerships with city councils and eco-conscious businesses seeking sustainable alternatives to traffic-congested truck deliveries. Consequently, CoopCycle promotes economic, social, and environmental sustainability, benefiting local economies and cooperatives alike.

Initially launched as a volunteer-driven grassroots initiative, CoopCycle began informally, leveraging community involvement and open-source technology to experiment with alternative logistics methods without substantial upfront investment. This volunteer-based start allowed CoopCycle to pilot its concept affordably and harness local expertise. As the initiative expanded in reach and influence, a more structured legal and financial framework became necessary.

While decentralization allows local cooperatives autonomy over decision-making, pricing strategies, and software customization, the growing size of the federation has introduced complexities. The need for balance between central coordination and local self-management is critical. To mitigate democratic strain caused by scale, CoopCycle has introduced a board of directors elected by its general assembly, enabling more streamlined decision-making while preserving democratic principles.

Today, CoopCycle is transitioning into a multi-stakeholder cooperative under French law, enabling collaboration among diverse economic actors committed to social and environmental goals. The cooperative encompasses eco-friendly businesses, zero-waste restaurants, family-owned social enterprises, local associations, municipalities, hospitals, and schools. This blend of organizational structure highlights a rich ecosystem within the social and solidarity economy, interacting dynamically with the traditional capitalist market. This evolution not only broadens CoopCycle's stakeholder coalition but also enhances its competitive position against conventional, profit-oriented platforms. This legal and organizational transformation is envisioned to foster inclusiveness, flexibility, and scalability while also enabling cross-sectoral collaborations beyond bike delivery. This transition positions CoopCycle as not only a provider of bike logistics but also a potential cooperative incubator capable of developing sustainable cross-sector value chains that align with broader post-capitalist ideals.

CoopCycle's future vision is to further develop the software and specialize in lobbying to expand the cooperative economy in France and beyond. CoopCycle seeks to occupy a niche of socio-economic activity and become sustainable in the short term, thus posing a potential threat for platform capitalism in the long term. CoopCycle's members are aware that establishing an anti-capitalist block presupposes the transformation of politics at a macro-institutional level (Borrits, 2019a, 2019b). One of the main challenges has been to harmonise centralisation with decentralisation and autonomy. Centralization zooms in the development of hard and heavy software (back-end), IT support, onboarding and training, collective bargaining (insurance, group purchasing), consultancy services sold to third-parties (Democracy at Work 2021), new partnerships for large commercial contracts (such as the

NHS) (Lowimpact TV 2020), APIs connection and lobbying. Decentralization zooms out to the autonomy of each member co-op to self-organize, customize the software and decide on marketing and pricing strategies. Against the centralized control of users' data by capitalist platforms, the CoopCycle's software decentralized logic means that it is self-hosted and self-administered by the local bike delivery co-ops. Yet, the expansion of CoopCycle into other countries has affected democratic processes. As an interviewee comments: "We are becoming too big to be fully democratic. Too many cities, too many projects, not enough time for people" (Interviewee). To tackle the problem, the federation has added an extra administrative layer, that is, a board of directors elected by the general assembly to represent member co-ops.

5.4. Circles UBI

Circles UBI[11] is a decentralized, blockchain-based sovereign credit currency operating within a web of trust (Figure 5.4). Unlike commodity-based money, which is typically backed by physical assets such as gold and determined by

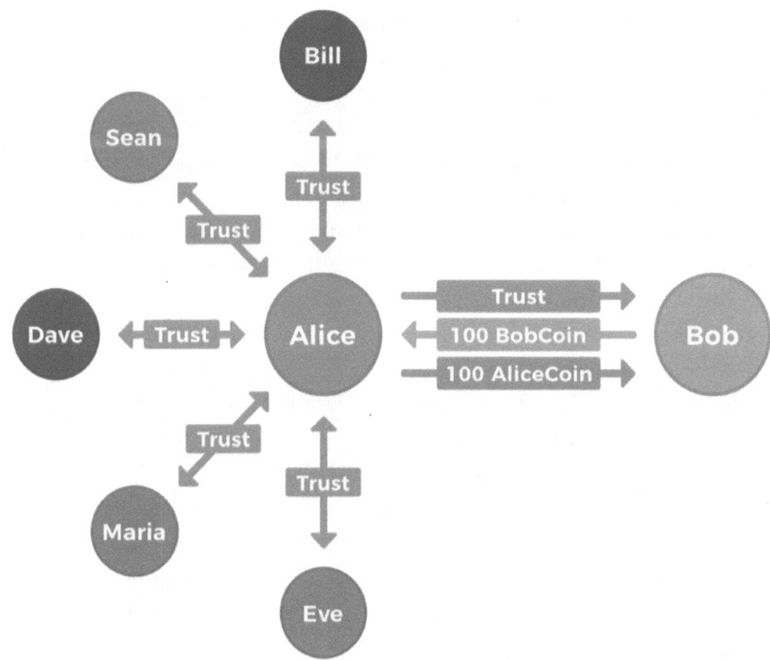

Figure 5.4. Circles UBI

11 https://www.circlesubi.id/

market forces and production factors, sovereign money draws its legitimacy from trust and political authority alone (Crocker 2020: 32–35). As such, sovereign money encompasses any form of currency supported by trust or political influence, including fiat money, cryptocurrencies, or community currencies.

Technically, Circles UBI is a protocol launched on the Gnosis Chain in October 2020 (Linares, 2023). Distinct from state-issued Universal Basic Income (UBI), Circles protocol issues ERC-20 tokens equally and unconditionally to individuals independently of nationality or state affiliation (Avanzo et al., 2023). Unlike other blockchain-based UBI initiatives designed as assets for profit accumulation, Circles functions primarily as a credit unit meant to settle debts based on mutual promises among participants.

The primary motivation behind Circles was to develop a more equitable and less centralized cryptocurrency compared to Bitcoin, integrating it with a political initiative to deliver a global universal basic income, ensuring basic necessities for everyone. This project entails a profound societal shift away from neocolonialism, exploitation, extraction, individualism, and work-centered values, towards ethics rooted in creativity, ecology, autonomy, self-sufficiency, community solidarity, care, and mutual support (Table 5.4). Consequently, money detaches itself from the commodity fetishism characteristic of Marxist reification and neoclassical utility.

Classical and neoclassical conceptions of value revolve around two main theories. The first is the labor or energy theory of value, which holds that value is ultimately determined by the amount of human labor or energy expended in production. From this perspective, value can only grow if more labor or energy is input. The second is the utility-based theory of value, in which value reflects the utility (or usefulness) a good provides—revealed through the prices individuals are willing to pay. However, neither the labor/energy theory nor the neoclassical utility theory has been empirically validated; neither can reliably predict market prices. In practice, it is impossible to measure the total labor or energy embedded in a good, or the utility it provides. As Sagoff (2008) notes, utility has never been independently measured to confirm its correlation with price or willingness to pay. If values are incommensurable, they cannot be aggregated, making it impossible to determine whether total value is increasing or not. Ultimately, value remains an inter-subjective construct, shaped by social conventions rather than measurable absolutes.

Circles UBI thus diverges from state-backed sovereign currencies, fiat money, or conventional credit systems, empowering communities instead through mutual credit networks that circulate values beyond profit maximization and capital accumulation (Cabaña and Linares, 2022).

Table 5.4. Discourses in Circles UBI

Value proposition	Governance	Economy	Law
UBI, blockchain, anticapitalism, anarchism, libertarianism, economic democracy **Problem**: nation-state centralized debt-based money supply and unfair capitalist distribution of money **Solution**: blockchain-based decentralized UBI Fair circular economy, money as a commons, solidarity, diversity, resilience, self-sustainability, change in the ethic of work	Direct democracy, monthly general assembly, decentralization, localism, democratic confederalism **Circles worker cooperative**: two full-time and eight part-time employees and several freelancers Executive board, core team meetings, online and in-person assembly, collective brainstorming, community hub, coordination group, working group, community reach out	Complementary currency, transparency, €2.3 million in donations, employee salaries R program in EUR for businesses participating in the Berlin pilot Community regulated exchange rates of CRC and fiat money Transaction fees covered by Gnosis Proposed 1/5 ratio between Circles credit and reserve capacity for B2B	Bylaws of Circles worker, cooperative Bits possessed collective Gnosis Chain, open-source software Circles wallet, seed phrase, public and private key Circles Safe: a smart contract that holds the keys to the accounts Transparency of transactions versus privacy (Entropy project)

> "Mutual credit systems point to the potential democratization of money, its creation, and its institutions—a money commons—a currency for the commons where credit is issued, co-owned, and administered by people democratically from the bottom-up rather than by state bureaucracies and banks (Cabaña and Linares, 2022)."

Circles UBI is a sort of a decentralized voting system that distributes reputation points across a web of trust in a digital marketplace and/or a local economy. The Circles standardized smart contract issues one Circles ERC-20 token (CRC) per hour for everyone who has an account in the network. To get an account, one needs to create a Circles Wallet and gain the trust of at least three trustees to start issuing. One can then spend or gain CRC by selling products or services. CRC cannot be exchanged for fiat or cryptocurrency but only for products and services. To become a buyer or a seller (private or business), one needs to register at the Circles Marketplace, which is the matchmaking infrastructure for resources and needs.

In February 2020, the Circles Co-op was founded to establish a flagship pilot program in Berlin, with the goal of implementing the Circles protocol within the local economy and fostering similar projects globally. The cooperative supported various groups and businesses interested in joining the Circles network. Its primary focus was on onboarding cooperatives, producers, and businesses whose services and products collectively address essential basic income needs, including food, healthcare, housing, and care services. Following its official launch in October 2020, the Circles network rapidly expanded globally, connecting over 100,000 individuals.

In July 2021, the Circles Co-op initiated a subsidy program for local businesses, enabling them to convert Circles tokens (CRCs) into euros (EUR). This initiative aimed to encourage a broader acceptance and circulation of CRCs within local supply chains by supporting diverse businesses. Participating enterprises included bicycle retailers and repair shops, cooperative bicycle distribution fleets, yoga and wellness studios, meditation and massage providers, small farms, cooperative supermarkets, local artisans and producers of beverages, clothing, and other goods, as well as additional service providers.

To prevent hoarding and incentivize economic activity, Circles UBI comes with an in-built deflationary monetary policy in the form of demurrage, which is a 7% annual decrease on all Circles balances. Inflation (an increase of 24 CRC/day or 8,760 CRC/year) and deflation (7% decrease per year) eventually cancel each other out in the course of approximately 14 years, meaning that every account would converge to around 125,143 CRC if they did not engage in any economic activity (buying or selling with CRC). The goal of demurrage is to increase the velocity of spending and ensure that over time there is a convergence between those who own more and those who own less CRC, thereby decreasing the disparity between those who join first and those who join later. Eventually, demurrage aims to engineer a fairer circular economy.

However, Circles faces structural challenges. Firstly, the concept of aligning individual incentives within the system proved complex, exemplified by the Berlin pilot experience. In this pilot, businesses received EUR subsidies intended to mitigate risks associated with accepting CRC as payment. Yet, the incentive structures revealed contradictions, as most participating businesses converted approximately 90% of their received CRC directly into EUR, using CRC merely as a stepping stone rather than actively circulating tokens within the local economy. Additionally, businesses converting CRC into EUR led to CRC-linked goods becoming perceived as luxury commodities due to limited practical usability, thereby undermining the project's intended economic inclusivity.

Further, significant technical challenges emerged. Blockchain-based issues such as constant smart contract bugs, problematic software upgrades, and persistent system errors disrupted the smooth functioning of the Circles platform both in Berlin and in ongoing implementations like the Bali pilot. Such technical obstacles made the system cumbersome for practical daily use, challenging its scalability and reliability. Complexities in the web-of-trust mechanisms, coupled with the scalability issues of blockchain technology, prevent the system from functioning smoothly at larger scales. Gnosis Chain's future efforts, such as developing Circles 2.0 and incorporating zero-knowledge proofs and group currencies, reflect attempts to address these concerns. These upgrades aim to simplify the user experience, enhance privacy, and enable Circles tokens to circulate more effectively in local economies, potentially creating closed-loop ecosystems that could strengthen cooperative supply chains and foster stronger community-based resilience. Ultimately, faced with these technical and economic complexities and contradictions inherent in attempting to build decentralized alternatives within a capitalist framework without direct state involvement, the Circles Co-op ended its operations in January 2024.

5.5. Subvert

Subvert[12] is not just a response to the decline of artist-focused platforms like Bandcamp—it's a bold, pragmatic reimagining of how platforms can function when built on collective ownership, democratic governance, and ethical technology. At its core, Subvert is a multi-sided digital marketplace where artists sell music and merchandise directly to supporters, but the operations behind this platform reflect a broader mission: to create a replicable framework for collectively owned internet services (Table 5.5).

Table 5.5. Subvert's business model

Value proposition	Governance	Economic policy	Law
A user-owned online multi-sided music marketplace Collective ownership Incentive alignment of investors and users Better financial tools, design, and community features	Heterarchical and democratic Ownership points (patronage) Membership classes: Artists, Labels, Supporters, Workers	Transaction fees Co-op membership dues Grants Equity fundraising via the corporation (not diluting co-op control)	A cooperative entity (limited cooperative association) A corporate entity (public benefit corporation)

12 https://subvert.fm/

Subvert seeks to directly confront several core failures of the current platform economy. Chief among these is the misalignment of incentives between users and owners—a structural flaw that often leads platforms to prioritize investor returns over user experience. This phenomenon, often described as "enshittification," results in platforms gradually extracting more value from their users while offering diminishing returns. Other issues include opaque governance, algorithmic manipulation, and a lack of transparency around how decisions are made—all of which leave users powerless and disillusioned. Subvert addresses these failures by embedding democratic participation and co-ownership into the architecture of the platform itself, ensuring that users are not only beneficiaries but decision-makers.

In the context of the music industry, Subvert tackles deeply entrenched problems that have long plagued independent artists and labels. Despite being central to the creation of cultural value, artists are often the last to be compensated fairly, sidelined by layers of intermediaries, exploitative contracts, and consolidated corporate control. The industry suffers from a lack of innovation, inadequate support for artist autonomy, and structural insecurity, as seen in recent sales and layoffs at platforms like Bandcamp. Artists find themselves vulnerable to abrupt policy changes and ownership transitions, with no say in decisions that directly affect their livelihoods. Subvert proposes a systemic solution by offering artists a stake in the platform they rely on, enabling them to retain control over their work, data, and revenue streams.

By realigning ownership and decision-making power with the communities who create value—artists, supporters, and workers—Subvert aims to transform the relationship between creators and the digital infrastructure they depend on. Its operational model isn't just an alternative; it's a prototype for a new paradigm in how cultural and economic value can be distributed more fairly and sustainably.

Subvert's organizational backbone is a dual-entity structure designed to balance cooperative control with access to traditional capital. At its core is Subvert Co-op, a Limited Cooperative Association owned entirely by its members—artists, supporters, labels, and platform workers—which builds and manages the platform. The Co-op wholly owns Subvert Corporation, structured as a C-Corp or Public Benefit Corporation, which holds the intellectual property and manages external investment. This bifurcated model allows Subvert to preserve member ownership and governance while engaging conventional fundraising mechanisms, including issuing preferred shares to investors.

Subvert's platform is designed to operate as both a digital marketplace and a cooperative governance system. It supports the sale of digital and physical music and merchandise with flexible pricing options, alongside built-in tools for automated revenue splitting among collaborators. The platform includes features for creator–supporter interaction, such as messaging, comments, and curated collections, intended to facilitate ongoing engagement. Member participation and economic rights are tracked through an Ownership Points system that represents a proportional cooperative stake based on activity and contribution, rather than tokenized assets. Governance functions are integrated directly into the platform, enabling members (artists, supporters, workers, labels) to vote, access records, and participate in decision-making as part of regular platform use.

Governance within Subvert is integrated into day-to-day operations through the cooperative structure. The Co-op is democratically controlled on a one-member-one-vote basis, with members participating in formal processes such as Board elections and bylaw changes, as well as informal mechanisms including nonbinding surveys and real-time feedback channels. In addition, Sounding Boards—interest-based working groups—provide members with opportunities to contribute to strategy, product development, and community initiatives. Subvert's governance framework is designed to be modular and capable of evolving over time. As the cooperative grows, the model may expand to incorporate mechanisms such as liquid democracy or delegate voting to support decision-making at scale, participatory budgeting to involve members in revenue allocation, and optional governance modules that can be adopted based on community needs, including features like ranked-choice voting or expedited decision processes. This approach allows governance practices to be adjusted incrementally in response to organizational complexity and member participation.

Subvert's strategic operations are structured with scalability in mind, using its legal and organizational framework as a template for launching additional collectively owned enterprises as the platform develops. Potential extensions of this ecosystem include services such as a vinyl pressing plant, a cooperative credit union, a housing cooperative, and physical spaces for work and performance. These ventures are intended to integrate with the existing structure, allowing for coordinated investment, shared infrastructure, and consistent approaches to ownership and governance across the broader cooperative network.

Subvert's financial operations are organized around its dual-entity structure, which separates cooperative governance from capital formation. Because the Co-op cannot issue traditional equity, the Corporation raises capital by issuing preferred shares, while the Co-op contracts with the Corporation for platform development and operational services. Revenue is generated through a combination of artist-selected, tiered sales commissions, cooperative membership fees, premium services, and optional higher platform fees that correspond to additional Platform Shares. This arrangement is intended to support financial sustainability while maintaining cooperative ownership and control. Subvert's cooperative structure allows for a broader range of approaches to financial sustainability and value distribution than conventional corporate models. Potential strategies include revenue-sharing dividends tied to Ownership Points and overall cooperative surplus, proportional payouts to contributors in the event of liquidity events or asset spin-offs, and the acceptance of grant or foundation funding that is typically inaccessible to standard for-profit entities. These mechanisms provide multiple pathways for aligning financial outcomes with member participation and long-term organizational goals.

Subvert's long-term strategy is framed as a range of possible scenarios that span self-sustained profitability with cooperative dividend distribution, investor buyouts that return full ownership to the Co-op, limited secondary liquidity for members, and structural outcomes such as nonprofit ownership, partial corporate sales, public listing with cooperative control, or nationalization as cultural infrastructure. The framework also includes more expansive possibilities, such as federating into a network of interconnected cooperatives or acquiring an existing platform like Bandcamp and transitioning it into a cooperative model. Together, these options outline a flexible approach to growth, liquidity, and long-term stewardship under collective governance. However, the platform is still at its early stage and the degree of its sustainability remains to be seen.

5.6. Transkribus

Transkribus,[13] operated by READ-COOP SCE, stands as a pioneering example of platform cooperativism in the realm of artificial intelligence (AI) and digital cultural heritage. Developed as a multi-stakeholder cooperative, Transkribus offers a platform for automated recognition and transcription of historical documents, leveraging AI to democratize access to cultural resources while embedding cooperative governance and commons-based at its core (Colutto et al., 2019; Mannan et al. 2026; Muehlberger et al., 2019; Terras et al., 2025).

Transkribus is a multi-sided platform that engages a user community comprising archivists, scholars, organizations, the public, and developers (Table 5.6). Individual users and organizations contribute training data (historical documents and transcripts), improving AI models and benefiting from increasingly accurate recognition tools. The platform's anti-rivalrous nature means that more contributions enhance the commons—in this case,

13 https://www.transkribus.org/

Table 5.6. Transkribus' business model

Value proposition	Governance	Economic policy	Law
Problem: manual page-by-page transcription of manuscripts is costly **Solution**: automated recognition and transcription of printed and handwritten documents Democratization of access to global cultural heritage (archives, historical documents, etc.)	Multi-stakeholder governance **Membership Classes**: Individuals (e.g., researchers, users), archives, universities, institutions, etc., external funders, platform contributors, governmental entities	Freemium Model Transcription credits Subscription fee for institutions Training and consulting services API licensing Machine learning and AI model licensing	European Cooperative Society READ-COOP SCE with limited liability open-source MIT licenses Public AI models

public domain commons such as historical documents—for all, exemplifying digital commons principles. Organizations can negotiate for large-scale, private AI models, generating additional revenue streams while supporting the broader commons through shared improvements.

READ-COOP SCE is registered as a European Cooperative Society (SCE), a legal form designed to support cross-border cooperative activity within the European Union. The cooperative includes more than 227 members across over 30 countries, encompassing universities, libraries, archives, and individual participants. This structure provides transnational legal recognition while embedding democratic governance and member control, generally following the principle of one member, one vote, with limited adaptations to accommodate legal entities.

READ-COOP's membership model is organized into distinct classes. Ordinary members, including both individuals and organizations, participate directly in governance and decision-making. Investing members, such as public authorities, are able to contribute capital but have capped voting rights to prevent disproportionate influence. In addition, employees and freelancers may become members, enabling them to participate in governance and align their labor with the cooperative's ownership and decision-making structure.

READ-COOP's approach to intellectual property and access combines open and proprietary elements. Certain components, such as the PyLaia HTR model, are released under open-source MIT licenses, while other parts of the platform remain proprietary in order to support financial sustainability.

The platform provides free access to more than 250 public AI models, and users retain ownership of their uploaded data and the resulting transcriptions. Access is structured through a freemium model in which non-members can use basic transcription services with a limited monthly credit allocation, while members and premium users receive expanded credits, additional features, and participation rights within the cooperative.

Governance and decision-making within READ-COOP are centered on the General Assembly, where members deliberate on issues such as pricing, elect directors, and influence strategic direction. Legal persons may hold up to five votes, while the voting power of investor members is capped at 25% of the total to limit disproportionate influence. The cooperative emphasizes transparency and accountability by allowing members to inspect financial statements, propose agenda items, and participate in annual conferences. At the same time, only a relatively small share of platform users are formal members, and comparatively high membership fees—reflecting significant operational costs—can present barriers to participation for smaller organizations, indicating room for more inclusive governance mechanisms.

READ-COOP's economic model is based on a combination of member share purchases, annual membership fees, and subscription revenues. This structure is designed to support significant infrastructure requirements, including the management of more than 400 terabytes of unique data and approximately 1.2 petabytes of storage, which necessitate a financially sustainable approach.

Several measures could strengthen governance and guide future development. Lowering barriers to membership, introducing user councils, and offering more flexible payment options could expand democratic participation beyond the current core membership. Establishing formal and transparent internal systems for dispute resolution would provide clearer pathways for addressing grievances and reinforce procedural fairness. In addition, more explicit communication about which components of the platform are open or proprietary, and the rationale behind these choices, could improve transparency and trust among users and members.

From a strategic perspective, aligning more explicitly with principles of open cooperativism could position Transkribus as a replicable model for other AI-driven commons initiatives that combine cooperative governance, sustainable business practices, and digital commons production. Increased partner-state and policy support—through public procurement, targeted funding, and legal recognition of cooperative digital infrastructures—could further enable this approach and contribute to a broader transition toward a commons-oriented digital economy.

Chapter 6

CROSS-CASE THEMATIC ANALYSIS AND DISCUSSION

Collectively, these case studies—P2P Lab/Tzoumakers, OFN, CoopCycle, Circles UBI, Subvert, Transkribus—attempt to apply the principles of cooperative organization and commons-based peer production across diverse sectors such as agriculture, manufacturing, e-logistics, food distribution, e-commerce, creative and cultural industries, and financial services. In doing so, they promote openness, sharing, transparency, self-governance, decentralization, and the equitable distribution of value among members. They leverage transformative technologies such as open-source software and hardware, the digital commons, and copyleft licenses to protect the commons and advance a post-capitalist, ethical, and sustainable economy.

The case studies constitute multi-stakeholder cooperative organizations that bear the characteristics of an open cooperative. They comprise civil society organizations producing material or immaterial commons, ethical market entities adding exchange value on top of the use value of the commons, and municipalities enabling public–commons partnerships. Municipalities, public authorities, and foundations prefigure the role of a partner-state. All case studies adopt multi-stakeholder governance, blending various models—from general assemblies and decentralized holacratic/sociocratic decision-making to more centralized federated structures.

The case studies integrate diverse financial strategies, including grants, crowdfunding, membership dues, service-based income, and solidarity-based exchanges. Rather than pursuing profit maximization, these initiatives prioritize equitable value distribution, reinvesting surplus into community-driven projects and infrastructure.

From a legal perspective, they adopt a mix of cooperative statutes, nonprofit entities, and foundation models, often navigating complex regulatory environments that do not always accommodate commons-oriented enterprises. Their legal approaches emphasize the use of copyleft and Creative Commons licenses to safeguard shared resources, while also advocating for policy reforms that recognize and institutionalize commons-based peer production. By experimenting with hybrid legal models, these initiatives seek to bridge the gap between existing legal constraints and the transformative potential of a post-capitalist economy.

However, they all face both context-specific and common challenges that constrain their capacity to scale, stabilize, and exert systemic impact. Across the cases, a recurring difficulty lies in achieving critical mass—whether in terms of users, contributors, or cooperative members—which limits network effects and long-term viability. P2P Lab/Tzoumakers faces difficulties clearly defining boundaries for collaboration, sustaining long-term community engagement in resource-intensive processes, and effectively coordinating globally dispersed contributors within open-source hardware production. OFN struggles with harmonizing diverse stakeholder interests across federated local entities, maintaining consistent ethical and operational standards, and ensuring coherent strategic decision-making across varying local contexts. CoopCycle experiences tensions between preserving local democratic control and managing global scalability, potentially risking internal conflicts and diluting cooperative identity.

Multi-stakeholder and participatory models must continuously negotiate tensions between inclusivity and efficiency, as well as between centralization and decentralization, particularly as initiatives grow. Circles UBI's Berlin pilot underscores governance issues such as building sufficient trust among participants, preventing misuse of unconditional digital tokens, and effectively embedding blockchain governance within comprehensive sociopolitical strategies necessary for systemic transformation. Subvert is still at an early stage, and it remains uncertain to what extent it can overcome the high switching costs and network effects that advantage established platforms such as Spotify and Bandcamp, each of which operates at a massive scale with millions of users. Transkribus could strengthen inclusivity by developing more accessible business models, such as introducing lower-cost subscription tiers, in order to reduce participation barriers for smaller organizations and individual users.

Economically, while public funding and donations play an enabling role, reliance on grants and project-based financing often undermines financial sustainability and exposes initiatives to discontinuity once funding cycles end. For P2P Lab and Tzoumakers, while their cosmolocalism model fosters decentralized production and open-source innovation, significant challenges include the financial and logistical complexity of scaling open-source hardware production. They also face difficulties bridging diverse stakeholder interests and securing long-term funding, potentially limiting their capacity to influence mainstream industrial practices. Tzoumakers also confront touristification and gentrification that threaten to turn the makerspace into a guesthouse. OFN encounters difficulties in achieving economic sustainability across decentralized entities, relying on fragmented revenue streams and risking limited market penetration due to competition from industrial food networks. CoopCycle struggles with financial viability amid intense market competition from well-funded capitalist platforms, risking cooperative sustainability due to dependency on membership fees and limited capital access. Circles UBI's economic model faces the critical issue of token volatility, ensuring stable purchasing power, preventing market speculation, and effectively integrating UBI within broader economic activities to ensure its usability and acceptance.

Legal and regulatory barriers further complicate development, especially in relation to hardware licenses, certification regimes, interoperability standards, and the recognition of open-source, cooperative, or commons-based organizational forms. OFN encounters regulatory challenges across jurisdictions, struggling to standardize cooperative statutes, navigate fragmented food industry regulations, and advocate policy changes that would institutionalize short food supply chains and digital commons within agricultural governance. CoopCycle's restrictive CoopyLeft licensing, while protective, limits scalability and potentially constrains collaboration beyond cooperative networks, creating tensions between openness and protection. Circles UBI faces critical regulatory uncertainties concerning blockchain-based currencies, compliance with financial laws, taxation, anti-money laundering policies, and legal recognition of blockchain-based mutual credit systems, which complicates its broader adoption and integration within established economic frameworks. Finally, these initiatives operate within broader structural contexts—such as platform capitalism, neoliberal agribusiness, and institutional inertia—that actively resist commons-oriented alternatives, making it difficult to align incentives, integrate with existing infrastructures, and translate experimental models into durable, large-scale transformations.

Across the case studies, it becomes clear that aligning incentives among multiple stakeholders is a central condition for cooperative business models to achieve long-term sustainability. Legal and financial innovations—such as Subvert's dual-entity structure and ownership points system—offer potential ways to address the capital constraints inherent in cooperatives while encouraging broader participation. Blockchain-based mutual credit systems like Circles could serve as liquidity injection mechanisms within commons-based economies, fostering resilience and ethical value distribution. However, this requires robust institutional partnerships and supportive public policies to overcome market pressures and the inertia of capitalist production systems. Complementary mechanisms, including copyfair licenses, data interoperability, and open standards, can further support the replication, coordination, and protection of shared digital infrastructures across supply chains within the cooperative economy. In this context, the digital commons functions as both a technological and institutional foundation for building resilient ecosystems of open cooperativism that seek to provide viable alternatives to extractive capitalist models.

Collectively, these case studies demonstrate the critical importance of embedding technological and cooperative innovations within broader political, economic, and social frameworks, emphasizing that successful implementation of their value propositions requires overcoming practical, structural, and strategic challenges inherent in pioneering a post-capitalist transition. Eventually, addressing these challenges requires a coordinated combination of institutional reforms, technological design choices, and viable business strategies. State financial and regulatory support, the development of cross-sectoral value propositions, inclusive governance and economic models aligning multi-stakeholder incentives, and innovative legal frameworks—alongside open sustainability standards—are all integral components of a counter-hegemonic strategy capable of fostering the transition toward a post-capitalist ethical, inclusive, and ecological economy.

Chapter 7

CONCLUSION

The model of open cooperativism, as explored throughout this book, represents a compelling and necessary response to the contemporary socio-economic challenges posed by platform capitalism, economic inequality, and environmental degradation. By merging the principles of commons-based peer production with cooperative governance and cosmolocalism, open cooperativism offers a transformative framework for reimagining economic organization beyond the constraints of neoliberal market logic.

7.1. Key Takeaways

The research and case studies examined—P2P Lab/Tzoumakers, OFN, CoopCycle, Circles UBI, Subvert.fm, and Transkribus—demonstrate that open cooperativism is not merely a theoretical construct but a viable model actively shaping economic alternatives. These initiatives showcase how digital commons, blockchain technology, multi-stakeholder governance, and cooperative legal structures can be harnessed to support economic resilience, inclusivity, and sustainability.

A few central conclusions emerge from this study:

1. **Value Proposition**

   Open cooperativism fosters decentralized cosmolocal production and open-source innovation, while prioritizing equitable value distribution—challenging the extractive tendencies of traditional capitalist enterprises. This is evident in how such initiatives generate and share economic, social, and environmental value.

   However, significant challenges arise, particularly in the financial and logistical complexity of scaling open-source hardware production and the long-term viability of relevant value propositions. Open cooperativism should build high-quality products coupled with a user-friendly experience that caters to both individual and collective needs and preferences.

2. Governance

Open cooperativism promotes multi-stakeholder governance, democratic decision-making, and consensus-based mechanisms. It draws on models such as direct democracy, liquid democracy, heterarchy, sociocracy, holacracy, and blockchain-enabled mechanisms like quadratic voting and conviction voting. These democratic processes reinforce the participatory and inclusive character of open cooperatives.

However, open cooperativism faces persistent challenges in aligning heterogeneous stakeholder interests and sustaining long-term community engagement, especially in resource-intensive processes. Issues such as voter apathy, conflicts of interest, and low member involvement can undermine its participatory ideals.

To address these obstacles, open cooperativism must better align incentives around collective ownership, fostering mutually beneficial partnerships among diverse stakeholders. The cases of Subvert and Transkribus illustrate how such alignment can support more resilient and collaborative governance models. Cosmolocal multi-level and multi-perspective institutional heterogeneity and complexity call for scaffolding levels of representative democracy and liquid democracy reconciling accountability and transparency, and large-scale coordination with efficiency, resilience and relocalization.

3. Economic Viability and Sustainability

One core economic advantage of utilizing common-pool resources for commons-based peer production is cost reduction, which marks the coopetitive advantage of open cooperativism vis-a-vis extractive capitalism. Yet, just like traditional and platform cooperativism, open cooperativism struggles to secure long-term funding, which can limit its influence on mainstream industrial practices. Commons-based peer production faces asymmetric competition with well-funded capitalist platforms. Challenges such as scalability, market competition, and regulatory barriers remain significant hurdles. These factors prevent open cooperativism from achieving critical mass.

To address these challenges, open cooperativism may adopt dual legal structures (e.g., as seen in Subvert) to attract external investment, while building strong value propositions and products around well-aligned, multi-stakeholder incentives. The so-called capital conundrum could be solved by a combination of state funding and innovative organizational structures that allow for friendly capital to be invested in multi-stakeholder partnerships supported by multisided platforms that apply Ostrom's design principles in cooperative frameworks as in the cases of Subvert and Transkribus.

4. Legal and Regulatory Challenges

Intellectual property rights, cooperative licensing models, and regulatory ambiguities present significant challenges for open cooperatives. Existing legal frameworks are often ill-suited to support the growth of commons-based enterprises, particularly those engaged in open-source hardware production.

Uncertainties around patent law, licensing options, and intellectual property rights expose open cooperatives to legal risks and complicate collaboration. Unlike software, hardware lacks mature, standardized open-source licensing models, making it harder to protect and share innovations while ensuring fair use.

To address these challenges, initiatives have emerged that propose alternative legal and governance tools. For example, the Copyfair license seeks to enable equitable sharing of value among contributors while protecting cooperative ownership. Open standards support interoperability and transparency, reducing dependency on proprietary systems. Platforms like Subvert offer replicable legal and technological infrastructures tailored to cooperative use, while tools such as the digital passport aim to ensure traceability, accountability, and compliance across distributed production networks.

Together, these approaches point toward a new legal and technical ecosystem better aligned with the principles of open cooperativism.

5. Post-Hegemony: Cross-Sectoral Collaboration

Partnerships between commons-based initiatives, ethical market actors, and public institutions are essential for scaling the impact of open cooperativism. Such collaborations can foster a broader ecosystem that supports the development of cooperative economies and the growth of digital commons.

To succeed, open cooperativism must embed its technological and cooperative innovations within wider political, economic, and social frameworks. The implementation of its value propositions is not only a technical or organizational task but also a structural and strategic challenge—one that involves navigating the complexities of a post-capitalist transition. This requires overcoming institutional inertia, market dominance by extractive platforms, and legal and financial barriers to alternative models of ownership and governance.

A promising approach lies in the concept of the partner state—a public institution that actively enables and co-produces commons-based and cooperative initiatives, rather than regulating them from above or outsourcing to private capital. Policy proposals aligned with this vision may include:

- Public procurement frameworks that prioritize cooperatives and open-source solutions.
- Funding and incubation programs for platform cooperatives and commons-oriented startups.
- Legal recognition and support for new forms of collective ownership and cooperative licensing.
- Infrastructure investment in open technologies and shared digital resources.
- Education and training policies that promote digital literacy, democratic governance, and cooperative entrepreneurship.

By aligning public policy with the goals of open cooperativism, the state can play a catalytic role in democratizing the economy, decentralizing power, and ensuring that innovation serves the many, not the few.

7.2. Challenges and Future Directions

Despite its transformative potential, open cooperativism faces several critical challenges that must be addressed to ensure its long-term viability and expansion.

1. **Scalability Without Dilution:** Many open cooperatives struggle to expand while maintaining their democratic and ethical principles. Strategies must be developed to scale operations without compromising core values.
2. **Capital and Financial Models:** Access to financing remains a pressing concern. Alternative funding mechanisms—such as cooperative crowdfunding, ethical investment funds, and government support—must be further explored and institutionalized.
3. **Regulatory Recognition and Policy Advocacy:** The legal status of open cooperatives needs further institutional recognition. Governments must be lobbied to create legal and financial infrastructures that support commons-based initiatives.
4. **Education and Capacity Building:** To expand the reach of open cooperativism, cooperative education programs and training initiatives should be widely implemented to empower communities and individuals to participate in cooperative governance and commons-based economies.

7.3. A Call to Action: Toward a Post-Capitalist Transition

The book has demonstrated that open cooperativism is not only a theoretical alternative but a practical and scalable economic model that aligns with principles of sustainability, inclusivity, and social justice. However, for this model to truly serve as a counter-hegemonic force against neoliberal capitalism, concerted efforts are required on multiple fronts—policy, finance, legal infrastructure, and grassroots mobilization. As Scholz (2023) emphasizes, the diversity of approaches in cooperativism demands a wide array of skills—from business and technological expertise to community organizing, cultural development, policy research, global coordination, and public advocacy. These efforts must be accompanied by both symbolic and practical actions that express solidarity, mutual support, and cooperation, all grounded in a shared commitment to collective goals.

As the global economy faces increasing crises—climate change, financial instability, and sociopolitical unrest—open cooperativism offers a radical yet pragmatic approach to reconfiguring economic systems in a way that prioritizes collective well-being over profit maximization. Through continued research, advocacy, and implementation, the ideals of open cooperativism can serve as a blueprint for a post-capitalist future where economic democracy, ecological responsibility, and social equity are at the forefront.

The transition from a market-driven to a commons-oriented economy will not happen overnight, nor will it be free from obstacles. Yet, the lessons drawn from the case studies in this book provide a foundation upon which future cooperative initiatives can build. If supported by a global network of activists, scholars, policymakers, and entrepreneurs, open cooperativism has the potential to redefine economic systems and create a truly sustainable and equitable world for future generations.

REFERENCES

Aigrain, P. (2012). *Sharing: Culture and the economy in the internet age.* Amsterdam University Press.

Altman, M. (2010). Cooperatives, history and theories of. In H. K. Anheier & S. Toepler (Eds.), *International encyclopedia of civil society.* Springer. https://doi.org/10.1007/978-0-387-93996-4_102.

Arrow, K. (1962). Economic welfare and the allocation of resources for invention. In R. Nelson (Ed.), *The rate and direction of inventive activity: Economic and social factors* (pp. 609–626). Princeton University Press.

Arvidsson, A., & Peitersen, N. (2013). *The ethical economy: Rebuilding value after the crisis.* Columbia University Press.

Avanzo, S. E., Criscione, T., Linares, J., & Schifanella, C. (2023, September). Universal basic income in a blockchain-based community currency. In Proceedings of the ACM International Conference on Information Technology for Social Good (GoodIT '23). Association for Computing Machinery. https://doi.org/10.1145/3582515.3609538.

Battilani, P., & Schröter, H. G. (Eds.). (2012). *The cooperative business movement, 1950 to the present.* Cambridge University Press. https://doi.org/10.1017/CBO9781139237208.

Bauwens, M. (2005). The political economy of peer production. *CTheory.*http://www.ctheory.net/articles.aspx?id=499.

Bauwens, M., & Kostakis, V. (2014). From the communism of capital to capital for the commons: Towards an open co-operativism. *tripleC: Communication, Capitalism & Critique,* 12(1), 356–361.

Bauwens, M., & Kostakis, V. (2017). Peer to peer production and the partner state. *Red Pepper.* http://www.redpepper.org.uk/peer-to-peer-production-and-the-partner-state

Bauwens, M., Kostakis, V., & Pazaitis, A. (2019). *Peer to peer: The commons manifesto.* University of Westminster Press.

Bauwens, M., & Niaros, V. (2017). *Value in the commons economy: Developments in open and contributory value accounting.* P2P Foundation.

Bauwens, M., & Pantazis, A. (2018). The ecosystem of commons-based peer production and its transformative dynamics. *The Sociological Review,* 66(2), 302–319. https://doi.org/10.1177/0038026118758532.

Benanav, A. (2020). *Automation and the future of work.* Verso.

Ben-Ner, A. (1984). On the stability of the cooperative form of organization. *Journal of Comparative Economics,* 8(3), 247–260. https://doi.org/10.1016/0147-5967(84)90027-3.

Benkler, Y. (2006). *The wealth of networks: How social production transforms markets and freedom.* Yale University Press.

Benkler, Y. (2013). Commons and growth: The essential role of open commons in market economies. *The University of Chicago Law Review,* 80(3), 1499–1555.

Birchall, J., & Ketilson, L. H. (2009). *Resilience of the cooperative business model in times of crisis.* International Labour Organization. https://www.ilo.org/sites/default/files/wcmsp5/groups/public/@ed_emp/@emp_ent/documents/publication/wcms_108416.pdf.

Birkinbine, B. J. (2020). *Incorporating the digital commons: Corporate involvement in free and open source software.* University of Westminster Press.

Bollier, D. (2003). *Silent theft: The private plunder of our common wealth.* Taylor & Francis.

Bollier, D. (2008). *Viral spiral: How the commoners built a digital republic of their own.* The New Press.

Bollier, D. (2014). *Think like a commoner: A short introduction to the life of the commons.* New Society Publishers.

Bollier, D., & Helfrich, S. (2012). *The wealth of the commons: A world beyond market and state.* Levellers Press.

Bollier, D., & Helfrich, S. (2019). *Free, fair and alive: The insurgent power of the commons.* New Society Publishers.

Borrits, B. (2019a, January 7). Coopcycle: Construire la qualification du métier contre le dumping social. *Association Autogestion.* https://autogestion.asso.fr/coopcycle-construire-la-qualification-du-metier-contre-le-dumping-social/.

Borrits, B. (2019b, January 16). *Nous sommes une start-up anarcho-communiste: Coopcycle auto-organise les coursiers à vélo.* Alternatives. https://basta.media/Nous-sommes-une-start-up-multinationale-anarcho-communiste-Coopcycle-auto.

Brown, W. (2015). *Undoing the demos: Neoliberalism's stealth revolution.* Zone Books.

Brynjolfsson, E., & McAfee, A. (2014). *The second machine age: Work, progress, and prosperity in a time of brilliant technologies.* W. W. Norton & Company.

Bunders, D. J., & De Moor, T. (2024). Paradoxical tensions as a double-edged sword: Analysing the development of platform cooperatives in the European gig economy. *Journal of Management Inquiry*, 33(4), 366–382. https://doi.org/10.1177/10564926231202422.

Cabaña, G., & Linares, J. (2022). Decolonising money: Learning from collective struggles for self-determination. *Sustainability Science*, 17(4), 1159–1170. https://doi.org/10.1007/s11625-022-01104-3.

Caffentzis, G., & Federici, S. (2014). Commons against and beyond capitalism. *Community Development Journal*, 49, 92–105.

Calzada, I. (2020). Platform and data co-operatives amidst European pandemic citizenship. *Sustainability*, 12(20), 8309. https://doi.org/10.3390/su12208309.

Castells, M. (2011). *The rise of the network society* (2nd ed.). Wiley-Blackwell.

Colutto, S., Kahle, P., Guenter, H., & Muehlberger, G. (2019). Transkribus: A platform for automated text recognition and searching of historical documents. In *2019 15th International Conference on eScience (eScience)* (pp. 463–466). IEEE. https://doi.org/10.1109/eScience.2019.00060.

Codagnone, C., Abadie, F., & Biagi, F. (2016a). *The future of work in the "sharing economy": Market efficiencies and equitable opportunities or unfair precarisation?* Joint Research Centre, Institute for Prospective Technological Studies. https://doi.org/10.2791/431485.

Codagnone, C., Biagi, F., & Abadie, F. (2016b). The passions and the interests: Unpacking the "sharing economy". Joint Research Centre, Institute for Prospective Technological *Studies.* https://doi.org/10.2791/474555.

CoopCycle. (n.d.). *Home.* https://coopcycle.org/en/.

Cornish, R. (2019). From farm gate to plate: How farmers are harnessing technology to bring food to your door. *Good Food.* https://www.smh.com.au/goodfood/farmers-are-doing-it-for-themselves-20190405-h1d7ko.html.

Crocker, G. (2020). Basic income and sovereign money. In *The alternative to economic crisis and austerity policy*. Palgrave Macmillan.

Crouch, C. (2004). *Post-democracy*. Polity Press.

Dardot, P., & Laval, C. (2017). *The new way of the world: On neoliberal society*. Verso.

Dardot, P., & Laval, C. (2014). *Commun: Essai sur la révolution au XXIe siècle*. La Découverte.

Davis, P. (2001). The governance of co-operatives under competitive conditions: Issues, processes and culture. *Corporate Governance*, 1(4), 28–39. https://doi.org/10.1108/EUM0000000005975.

De Angelis, M. (2017). *Omnia sunt communia: On the commons and the transformation to postcapitalism*. Zed Books.

De Lautour, V. J., & Cortese, L. C. (2016). Cooperatives: Governance and accountability systems for a better world? *Journal of Accounting and Organisational Change*, 12(1), 1–9.

Dean, J. (2009). *Democracy and other neoliberal fantasies: Communicative capitalism and left politics*. Duke University Press.

Dean, J. (2012). *The communist horizon*. Verso.

De Filippi, P., Mannan, M., & Reijers, W. (2024). Blockchain technology and the rule of code: Regulation via governance. *HAL Open Science*. https://hal.science/hal-03883249.

Democracy at Work. (2021). *All things co-op: CoopCycle [Video]*. YouTube. https://www.youtube.com/watch?v=26qCKUjS9go&t=21s.

Dow, G. K. (2003). Governing the firm: Workers' control in theory and practice. *Cambridge University Press*. https://doi.org/10.1017/CBO9780511498746.

Dufresne, A., & Leterme, C. (2021). App workers united: The struggle for rights in the gig economy. *GUE/NGL-The Left in the European Parliament*. https://left.eu/content/uploads/2021/02/Study_EMPL2-v2-App.pdf.

Dyer-Witheford, N. (1999). *Cyber-Marx: Cycles and circuits of struggle in high-technology capitalism*. University of Illinois Press.

Dyer-Witheford, N. (2015). *Cyber-proletariat: Global labour in the digital vortex*. Pluto Press.

Eurofound. (2018). *Employment and working conditions of selected types of platform work*. Publications Office of the European Union. https://assets.eurofound.europa.eu/f/279033/bd2948158a/ef18001en.pdf.

Fakhfakh, F., Pérotin, V., & Gago, M. (2012). Productivity, capital, and labor in labor-managed and conventional firms in France. *Industrial and Labor Relations Review*, 65(4), 847–879. https://doi.org/10.1177/001979391206500407.

Federici, S. (2004). *Caliban and the witch: Women, the body and primitive accumulation*. Autonomedia.

Federici, S. (2012). *Revolution at point zero: Housework, reproduction, and feminist struggle*. PM Press.

Ferraro, F., Pfeffer, J., & Sutton, R. I. (2005). Economics language and assumptions: How theories can become self-fulfilling. *Academy of Management Review*, 30(1), 8–24.

Fiss, P. C. (2009). Case studies and the configurational analysis of organizational phenomena. In D. Byrne & C. C. Ragin (Eds.), *The SAGE handbook of case-based methods* (pp. 424–440). SAGE.

Fourier, C. (1971). *The theory of the four movements* (G. Stedman Jones & I. Patterson, Trans.). Cambridge University Press. (Original work published 1808).

Foster, S. R., & Iaione, C. (2019). The city as a commons. *Yale Law & Policy Review*, 34(2), 281–349.

Frenken, K., van Waes, A., Pelzer, P., Smink, M., & van Est, R. (2020). Safeguarding public interests in the platform economy. *Policy and Internet*, 12(5), 400–425. https://doi.org/10.1002/poi3.217.

Freund, A., & Stanko, D. (2018). The wolf and the caribou: Coexistence of decentralized economies and competitive markets. *Journal of Risk and Financial Management*, 11(2), Article 26. https://doi.org/10.3390/jrfm11020026.

Fuchs, C. (2014). *Digital labour and Karl Marx*. Routledge.

Fuchs, C. (2022). *Digital capitalism: Media, communication and society* (2nd ed.). Routledge.

Furubotn, E. G., & Pejovich, S. (1970). Property rights and the behavior of the firm in a socialist state: The example of Yugoslavia. *Zeitschrift für Nationalökonomie*, 30(3–4), 431–454. https://doi.org/10.1007/BF01289247.

Fuster Morell, M., & Espelt, R. (2018, August). How much are digital platforms based on open collaboration? An analysis of technological and knowledge practices and their implications for the platform governance of a sample of 100 cases of collaborative digital platforms in Barcelona. In Proceedings of the 14th International Symposium on Open Collaboration (OpenSym '18). Association for Computing Machinery. https://doi.org/10.1145/3233391.3233970.

Gershenfeld, N. (2007). *Fab: The coming revolution on your desktop—From personal computers to personal fabrication*. Basic Books.

Gibbert, M., Ruigrok, W., & Wicki, B. (2008). What passes as a rigorous case study? *Strategic Management Journal*, 29(13), 1465–1474.

Giotitsas, C. (2019). *Open source agriculture: Grassroots technology in the digital era*. Palgrave Macmillan.

Giotitsas, C., & Ramos, J. (2017). A *new model of production for a new economy*. P2P Foundation.

Graham, J., & Gibson, K. (1996). *The end of capitalism (as we knew it): A feminist critique of political economy*. University of Minnesota Press.

Graham, J., & Gibson, K. (2006). *A postcapitalist politics*. University of Minnesota Press.

Graham, M., & Shaw, J. (Eds.). (2017). *Towards a fairer gig economy*. Meatspace Press. http://www.relats.org/documentos/FT.SIND.GU.UNIgigeconomy.pdf.

Griffiths, T. (2008). *Techniques of governance in commons based peer production*. School of Culture and Communication, University of Melbourne.

Guttmann, A. (2021). Commons and cooperatives: A new governance of collective action. *Annals of Public and Cooperative Economics*, 92(2), 247–268. https://doi.org/10.1111/apce.12291.

Hardt, M., & Negri, A. (2000). *Empire*. Harvard University Press.

Hardt, M., & Negri, A. (2004). *Multitude: War and democracy in the age of empire*. Penguin.

Hardt, M., & Negri, A. (2009). *Commonwealth*. Belknap Press.

Heidegger, M. (1977). *The question concerning technology and other essays* (W. Lovitt, Trans.). Garland Publishing.

Hess, C., & Ostrom, E. (Eds.). (2007). U*nderstanding knowledge as a commons: From theory to practice*. MIT Press.

Howe, J. (2006, June). *The rise of crowdsourcing*. Wired. https://www.wired.com/2006/06/crowds/.

Hueth, B. (2014, September 4). *Missing markets and the cooperative firm. Paper presented at the Workshop on Producers' Organizations in Agricultural Markets*, Toulouse, France.

Huws, U. (2003). *The making of a cybertariat: Virtual work in a real world*. Monthly Review Press.

Huws, U. (2014). *Labor in the global digital economy: The cybertariat comes of age*. Monthly Review Press.

Huws, U., Spencer, N. H., Syrdal, D. S., & Holts, K. (2018). *Work in the European gig economy: Research results from the UK, Sweden, Germany, Austria, The Netherlands, Switzerland and Italy*. FEPS, UNI Europa, University of Hertfordshire. https://uhra.herts.ac.uk/bitstream/handle/2299/19922/Huws_U._Spencer_N.H._Syrdal_D.S._Holt_K._2017_.pdf.

International Cooperative Alliance & Euricse. (2023). *Exploring the cooperative economy: World cooperative monitor 2023 report*. International Cooperative Alliance. https://monitor.coop.

International Co-operative Alliance. (2014). *Cooperative identity, values and principles*. https://www.ica.coop/en/cooperatives/cooperative-identity.

International Labour Organization. (2022). *Measuring cooperatives: An information guide on the ILO guidelines concerning statistics of cooperatives*. International Labour Organization.

Jarzębowski, S., Bourlakis, M., & Bezat-Jarzębowska, A. (2020). Short food supply chains (SFSC) as local and sustainable systems. *Sustainability*, 12(11), 4715.

Jensen, A., & McDonnell, D. (2019). *Worker cooperatives and firm performance: A meta-analysis. Economic and Industrial Democracy*. Advance online publication. https://doi.org/10.1177/0143831X19840853.

Joyce, S., Stuart, M., & Forde, C. (2022). Theorising labour unrest and trade unionism in the platform economy. *New Technology, Work and Employment*, 37(3), 383–399. https://doi.org/10.1111/ntwe.12252.

Kallis, G. (2018). *Degrowth*. Agenda Publishing.

Kasparian, D. (2022). CoopCycle in Argentina. *Grassroots Economic Organising*. https://geo.coop/articles/coopcycle-argentina.

Kioupkiolis, A. (2019). *The common and counter-hegemonic policies*. Edinburgh University Press.

Kioupkiolis, A. (2017). Commoning the political, politicising the common: Community and the political in Jean-Luc Nancy, Roberto Esposito and Giorgio Agamben. *Contemporary Political Theory*, 17(3), 283–305.

Kioupkiolis, A. (2021). Digital commons, the political and social change: Towards an integrated strategy of counter-hegemony furthering the commons. *ephemera*. http://www.ephemerajournal.org/contribution/digital-commons-political-and-social-change-towards-integrated-strategy-counter.

Kioupkiolis, A. (2023). *Common hegemony, populism, and the new municipalism: Democratic alter-politics and transformative strategies*. Routledge.

Kostakis, V. (2018). In defence of digital commoning. *Organization*, 25(6), 812–818.

Kostakis, V., & Bauwens, M. (2014). *Network society and future scenarios for a collaborative economy*. Palgrave Macmillan.

Kostakis, V., Niaros, V., Dafermos, G., & Bauwens, M. (2015). Design global, manufacture local: Exploring the contours of an emerging productive model. *Futures*, 73, 126–135.

Kostakis, V., Latoufis, K., Liarokapis, M., & Bauwens, M. (2016). The convergence of digital commons with local manufacturing from a degrowth perspective: Two illustrative cases. *Journal of Cleaner Production*. https://doi.org/10.1016/j.jclepro.2016.09.077.

Kostakis, V., Pazaitis, A., & Liarokapis, M. (2023). Beyond high-tech versus low-tech: A tentative framework for sustainable urban data governance. *Big Data & Society*, 10(1). https://doi.org/10.1177/20539517231180583.

Kuhn, T. S. (1962). *The structure of scientific revolutions*. University of Chicago Press.

Laclau, E. (2005). *On populist reason*. Verso.

Laclau, E., & Mouffe, C. (2001). *Hegemony and socialist strategy: Towards a radical democratic politics*. Verso.

Lapavitsas, C. (2022). *The state of capitalism: Economy, society, and hegemony*. Verso.

Latour, B. (1992). Where are the missing masses? The sociology of a few mundane artifacts. In W. E. Bijker & J. Law (Eds.), *Shaping technology/building society* (pp. 225–258). MIT Press.

Lessig, L. (2001). *The future of ideas: The fate of the commons in a connected world.* Random House.

Lessig, L. (2004). *Free culture.* Penguin.

Linares, J. (2023). Basic income in local currencies. In M. Torry (Ed.), *The Palgrave international handbook of basic income* (pp. 254–261). Palgrave Macmillan.

Lowimpact TV. (2020). *CoopCycle federation: A bicycle courier co-op in every town [Video].* YouTube. https://www.youtube.com/watch?v=Q6hzXcLda-U&t=671s.

Malta, M. C., Bandeira, A. M., Bertuzi, R., Castro, C., Meira, D., Pereira, D., Pereira, I., Vieira, I., & Tomé, B. (2020). A framework for cooperatives' transparency: A linked data approach. *Congreso Internacional de Investigadores en Economía Social y Cooperativa.* http://ciriec.es/wp-content/uploads/2020/09/COMUN-087-T16-CURADO-BANDEIRA-et-al-ok.pdf.

Mannan, M., Wong, J., & Bietti, E. (2022). Data cooperatives in Europe: A preliminary investigation. *Network Industries Quarterly*, 24(3), 12–15.

Mannan, M., & Pek, S. (2024). Platform cooperatives and the dilemmas of platform worker-member participation. *New Technology, Work and Employment*, 39(2), 219–237. https://hdl.handle.net/1814/75688.

Mannan, M., Pek, S., & Papadimitropoulos, V. (2026). The cooperative governance of artificial intelligence: The case of READ-COOP's Transkribus platform. In J. N. Warren, K. Ogunyemi, A. Guerreschi, & M. Szulc (Eds.), *Global cooperative economics and movements: A research companion.* Routledge.

Markard, J., Raven, R., & Truffer, B. (2012). Sustainability transitions: An emerging field of research and its prospects. *Research Policy*, 41(6), 955–967. https://doi.org/10.1016/j.respol.2012.02.013.

Marx, K. (1973). *Grundrisse: Foundations of the critique of political economy (Rough draft)* (M. Nicolaus, Trans.). Penguin Books. (Original work written 1857–1858).

Mayo, E. (2019). Digital democracy? Options for the International Cooperative Alliance to advance platform coops. *International Co-operative Alliance.* https://www.uk.coop/sites/default/files/2020-11/annex_1_-_digital_democracy_discussion_paper_-_en.pdf.

Micheli, M., Ponti, M., Craglia, M., & Berti Suman, A. (2020). Emerging models of data governance in the age of datafication. *Big Data & Society*, 7(2).

Miyazaki, H. (1984). On success and dissolution of the labor-managed firm in the capitalist economy. *Journal of Political Economy*, 92(5), 909–931. https://doi.org/10.1086/261268.

Morell, M. F. (2010). *Governance of online creation communities: Provision of infrastructure for the building of digital commons (Doctoral dissertation*, European University Institute). European University Institute.

Morozov, E. (2018). From Airbnb to city bikes, the "sharing economy" has been seized by big money. *The Guardian.*https://www.theguardian.com/commentisfree/2018/nov/27/airbnb-city-bikes-sharingeconomy-big-money.

Mohamad, M., Othman, W. I., & Mohamed, A. (2013). Accountability issues and challenges: The scenario for Malaysian cooperative movement. *World Academy of Science, Engineering and Technology International Journal of Economics and Management Engineering*, 7(6).

Mouffe, C. (2000). *The democratic paradox.* Verso.

Mouffe, C. (2005). *On the political.* Verso.

Muehlberger, G., Seaward, L., Terras, M., Oliveira, S. A., Bosch, V., Bryan, M., Colutto, S., Déjean, H., Diem, M., Fiel, S., Gatos, B., Greinoecker, A., Grüning, T., Hackl, G., Haukkovaara, V., Heyer, G., Hirvonen, L., Hodel, T., Jokinen, M., Kahle, P., Kallio, M., Kaplan, F., Kleber, F., Labahn, R., Lang, E. M., Laube, S., Leifert, G.,

Louloudis, G., McNicholl, R., Meunier, J.-L., Michael, J., Mühlbauer, E., Philipp, N., Pratikakis, I., Puigcerver Pérez, J., Putz, H., Retsinas, G., Romero, V., Sablatnig, R., Sánchez, J. A., Schofield, P., Sfikas, G., Sieber, C., Stamatopoulos, N., Strauß, T., Terbul, T., Toselli, A. H., Ulreich, B., Villegas, M., Vidal, E., Walcher, J., Weidemann, M., Wurster, H., & Zagoris, K. (2019). Transforming scholarship in the archives through handwritten text recognition: Transkribus as a case study. *Journal of Documentation*, 75(5), 954–976. https://doi.org/10.1108/JD-07-2018-0114.

Muldoon, J. (2022). *Platform socialism*. Pluto Press.

Murdock, G. (2013). Communication in common: Historical and normative foundations of communication research. *International Journal of Communication*, 7, 154–172.

Niaros, V., Kostakis, V., & Drechsler, W. (2017). Making (in) the smart city: The emergence of makerspaces. *Telematics and Informatics*, 34, 1143–1152.

Open Food Network. (n.d.). *OFN handbook*. https://ofn-user-guide.gitbook.io/ofn-handbook/.

Ortolan, M. (2020, May 22). *Violet Town farmers find global success during coronavirus pandemic*. ABC News. https://www.abc.net.au/news/2020-05-22/violet-town-farmers-global-success-duringcoronavirus-pandemic/12276162.

Ossewaarde, M., & Reijers, W. (2017). The illusion of the digital commons: "False consciousness" in online alternative economies. *Organization*, 24(5), 609–628.

Ostrom, E. (1990). *Governing the commons: The evolution of institutions for collective action*. Cambridge University Press.

Ostrom, E. (2000). Collective action and the evolution of social norms. *Journal of Economic Perspectives*, 14(3), 137–158.

Owen, R. (1991). *A new view of society and other writings* (G. Claeys, Ed.). Penguin Books. (Original work published 1813–1816)

Pantazis, A., & Meyer, M. (2020). Tools from below: Making agricultural machines convivial. *The Greek Review of Social Research*, 155, 39–58.

Papadimitropoulos, V. (2017). The politics of the commons: Reform or revolt? *tripleC: Communication, Capitalism & Critique*, 15(2), 563–581.

Papadimitropoulos, V. (2019). Politics and the political. *Critical Horizons*, 20(1), 40–53.

Papadimitropoulos, V. (2020). *The commons: Economic alternatives in the digital age*. University of Westminster Press.

Papadimitropoulos, V. (2023). *Blockchain and the commons*. Routledge.

Papadimitropoulos, V. (2023). The digital commons, cosmolocalism, and open cooperativism: The cases of P2P Lab and Tzoumakers. *Organization*, 0(0). https://doi.org/10.1177/13505084231156268.

Papadimitropoulos, V., & Malamidis, H. (2023). Prefiguring the counter-hegemony of open cooperativism: The case of Open Food Network. *Journal of Rural Studies*, 101, Article 103067. https://doi.org/10.1016/j.jrurstud.2023.103067.

Papadimitropoulos, V., & Malamidis, H. (2024). The transformative potential of platform cooperativism: The case of CoopCycle. tripleC: Communication, Capitalism *& Critique*, 22(1), 1–24. https://doi.org/10.31269/triplec.v22i1.1418.

Papadimitropoulos, V., & Perperidis, G. (2024). Universal basic income on blockchain: The case of Circles UBI. *Frontiers in Blockchain*, 7, Article 1362939. https://doi.org/10.3389/fbloc.2024.1362939.

Pazaitis, A., & Drechsler, W. (2021). Peer production and state theory: Envisioning a cooperative partner state. In M. O'Neil, C. Pentzold, & S. Toupin (Eds.), *The handbook of peer production* (pp. 359–370). Wiley-Blackwell. https://www.wiley.com/en-au/The+Handbook+of+Peer+Production-p-9781119537090.

Pazaitis, A., Kostakis, V., & Bauwens, M. (2017). Digital economy and the rise of open cooperativism: The case of the Enspiral Network. *Transfer: European Review of Labour and Research*, 23(2), 177–192. https://doi.org/10.1177/1024258916683865.

Pinch, T. J., & Bijker, W. E. (2012). The social construction of facts and artifacts: Or how the sociology of science and the sociology of technology might benefit each other. In W. Bijker, T. P. Hughes, & T. Pinch (Eds.), *The social construction of technological systems: New directions in the sociology and history of technology* (pp. 11–44). MIT Press.

Proudhon, P.-J. (1994). *What is property?* (D. R. Kelley & B. G. Smith, Trans.). Cambridge University Press. (Original work published 1840)

Puri, D. L., & Walsh, J. (2018). Impact of good governance on performance of cooperatives in Nepal. *Management and Marketing*, 16(2).

Rawls, J. (1971). *A theory of justice.* Harvard University Press.

Restakis, J. (2010). *Humanizing the economy: Co-operatives in the age of capital.* New Society Publishers.

Riders Collective. (2021). *Cooperatives – HOW TO? – The CoopCycle model [Video].* YouTube. https://www.youtube.com/watch?v=OGYoyB-rrjg.

Rifkin, J. (2014). *The zero marginal cost society: The internet of things, the collaborative commons, and the eclipse of capitalism.* Palgrave Macmillan.

Rigi, J. (2014). The coming revolution of peer production and revolutionary cooperatives: A response to Michel Bauwens, Vasilis Kostakis and Stefan Meretz. tripleC: Communication, Capitalism *& Critique*, 12(1), 390–404.

Rozas, D., Tenorio-Fornés, A., & Hassan, S. (2021). Analysis of the potentials of blockchain for the governance of global digital commons. *Frontiers in Blockchain*, 4, Article 577680. https://doi.org/10.3389/fbloc.2021.577680.

Rushkoff, D. (2016). *Throwing rocks at the Google bus: How growth became the enemy of prosperity.* Portfolio/Penguin.

Sagoff, M. (2008). *The economy of the Earth: Philosophy, law, and the environment* (2nd ed.). Cambridge University Press.

Sandoval, M. (2020). Entrepreneurial activism? Platform cooperativism between subversion and co-optation. *Critical Sociology*, 46(6), 801–817. https://doi.org/10.1177/0896920519870577.

Schlager, E., & Ostrom, E. (1992). Property-rights regimes and natural resources: A conceptual analysis. *Land Economics*, 68(3), 249–262. https://doi.org/10.2307/3146375

Scholz, T. (2023). *Own this!: How platform cooperatives help workers build a democratic internet.* Verso Books.

Scholz, T. (2016). *Platform cooperativism: Challenging the corporate sharing economy.* Rosa Luxemburg Stiftung.

Scholz, T., & Schneider, N. (Eds.). (2016). *Ours to hack and to own: The rise of platform cooperativism: A new vision for the future of work and a fairer internet.* OR Books.

Scholz, T., Mannan, M., Pentzien, J., & Plotkin, H. (2021). *Policies for cooperative ownership in the digital economy.* Berggruen Institute. https://www.berggruen.org/ideas/articles/policies-for-cooperative-ownership-in-the-digital-economy/.

Simon, H. W. (2019). Economic democracy and enterprise form in finance. *Politics and Society*, 47(4), 557–571.

Smith, A. (2007). Translating sustainabilities between green niches and socio-technical regimes. *Technology Analysis & Strategic Management*, 19(4), 427–450. https://doi.org/10.1080/09537320701403334.

Smyrnaios, N. (2018). *Internet oligopoly: The corporate takeover of our digital world.* Emerald Publishing.

Söderberg, J. (2008). *Hacking capitalism: The free and open source software movement.* Routledge.

Spier, S. (2022). *The ethics and politics of platform cooperatives.* Institute for Digital Cooperative Economy. https://ia802203.us.archive.org/8/items/shakedspier/Shaked%20Spier%20%28Mar%2014%29.pdf.

Spear, R. (2000). The cooperative advantage. *Annals of Public and Cooperative Economics,* 71(4), 507–523. https://doi.org/10.1111/1467-8292.00152.

Srnicek, N. (2017). *Platform capitalism.* Polity Press.

Stalder, F. (2005). *Open cultures and the nature of networks.* New Media Center_kuda.org.

Stallman, R. (2002). *Free software, free society.* GNU Press.

Standing, G. (2011). *The precariat: The new dangerous class.* Bloomsbury Academic.

Stiglitz, J. E. (2008). Economic foundations of intellectual property rights. *Duke Law Journal,* 57(6), 1693–1724.

Stiglitz, J. E. (2012). *The price of inequality: How today's divided society endangers our future.* W. W. Norton & Company.

Summers, L. H. (2014). U.S. economic prospects: Secular stagnation, hysteresis, and the zero lower bound. *Business Economics,* 49(2), 65–73. https://doi.org/10.1057/be.2014.13.

Terras, M., Anzinger, B., Gooding, P., Mühlberger, G., Nockels, J., Romein, C. A., Stauder, A., & Stauder, F. (2025). The artificial intelligence cooperative: READ-COOP, Transkribus, and the benefits of shared community infrastructure for automated text recognition. Open Research *Europe,* 5(16). https://doi.org/10.12688/openreseurope.18747.1.

Toffler, A. (1980). *The third wave.* William Morrow.

Troxler, P. (2010). Commons-based peer-production of physical goods: Is there room for a hybrid innovation ecology? Paper presented at the 3rd Free Culture Research Conference, Berlin, Germany. https://ssrn.com/abstract=1692617.

UNCTAD. (2019). *Digital economy report 2019: Value creation and capture: Implications for developing countries.* United Nations. https://unctad.org/system/files/official-document/der2019_en.pdf.

Van Doorn, N. (2017). Platform cooperativism and the problem of the outside. *Culture Digitally.* https://culturedigitally.org/2017/02/platformcooperativism-and-the-problem-of-the-outside.

Vanek, J. (1977). *The labor-managed economy: Essays by Jaroslav Vanek.* Cornell University Press.

Varoufakis, Y. (2020). *Another now: Dispatches from an alternative present.* The Bodley Head.

Varoufakis, Y. (2023). *Technofeudalism: What killed capitalism.* The Bodley Head.

Wagner, R. P. (2003). Information wants to be free: Intellectual property and the mythologies of control. Columbia Law Review, 103. https://ssrn.com/abstract=419560.

Wallace, D. I. (2026). Australian platform cooperative case study: The Open Food Network. In *Exploring Asian-Pacific co-operatives in theory and practice* (pp. 369–378). Elsevier. https://doi.org/10.1016/B978-0-443-23784-3.00007-7.

Ward, B. (1958). The firm in Illyria: Market syndicalism. *The American Economic Review,* 48(4), 566–589.

Weber, S. (2004). *The success of open source.* Harvard University Press.

Winner, L. (2020). *The whale and the reactor: A search for limits in an age of high technology.* University of Chicago Press.

Woodcock, J. (2020). The algorithmic panopticon at Deliveroo: Measurement, precarity, and the illusion of control. *Ephemera: Theory and Politics in Organisation*, 20(3), 67–95. https://ephemerajournal.org/contribution/algorithmic-panopticondeliveroo-measurement-precarity-and-illusion-control-0.

Wright, E. O. (2009). *Envisioning real utopias.* Verso.

Yin, R. K. (2014). *Case study research: Design and methods* (5th ed.). SAGE.

Žižek, S. (2008). *In defense of lost causes.* Verso.

Žižek, S. (2010). How to begin from the beginning. In C. Douzinas & S. Žižek (Eds.), *The idea of communism* (pp. 209–226). Verso.

INDEX

agroecology 38
algorithmic management 13
alternative economic models 3, 33
anti-capitalism 8, 21, 41, 42
automation and work 2, 49, 50, 51

basic income (UBI) 2, 4, 29, 44, 46
Bauwens, Michel 2, 3, 8, 10, 18, 22
Benkler, Yochai 8–10
blockchain and governance 2, 7, 10, 45, 54, 55, 57, 58
business models of platform cooperatives 12, 24, 28

capitalism, critique of 17
Circles UBI 2, 4, 29, 43–47, 53, 54, 55, 57
climate change and economic models 5, 35, 61
commons and digital economy 1, 5, 12, 52
commons-based peer production 2–10, 22–24, 27–29, 31, 53, 57, 58
community-based cooperatives 47
CoopCycle 2, 4, 9, 13, 29, 39–43, 53–55, 57
cooperative governance 2, 4, 48–50, 52, 57, 60
cross-case analysis 30
cryptocurrency and economic alternatives 44, 45
cyber-marxism 5

degrowth 10
digital commons 1–7, 9–11, 21–24, 28, 29, 38, 39, 51–53, 55–57, 59
digital democracy 60
Distributed Autonomous Organizations (DAOs) 6, 7

economic democracy 24, 27, 61
environmental sustainability 23, 41
equitable value distribution 9, 41, 53, 57
ethical market entities 3, 18, 22, 23, 26–28, 34, 35, 53

feminist economics 24
financial models for cooperatives 60
Food Networks, Open 2, 4, 29, 35–39
free software and cooperatives 2, 5, 7, 9, 10, 39, 53

gig economy critique 39
governance models 2, 27, 35, 58
green capitalism 9

hegemony, counter 25, 28, 30
historical development of cooperatives 7, 26

intellectual property and cooperatives 4, 7, 10, 23, 48, 51, 59
intercooperation among cooperatives 16, 22

just transition 3, 61

knowledge sharing and commons 7

labor and digital platforms 5, 6, 13
law and cooperatives 4, 30, 42
localized production models 2, 57

methodology of case studies 29
Mondragon corporation 16
mutual aid and cooperatives 13–14, 24, 58

neoliberalism and digital economy 5, 6, 28
network governance 35, 37

open access knowledge 7, 9
open cooperativism 1–61
Open Food Network 2, 4, 29, 35–39, 53–55, 57
Ostrom, Elinor 1, 3, 8–10, 21, 34, 58

P2P Lab and Tzoumakers 2, 3, 29, 31–33, 53, 54, 57
participatory budgeting 27, 49
partner state and commons 3, 18, 26–28, 53, 59
platform capitalism *vs.* cooperativism 18
platform cooperativism 1–3, 6, 9, 12, 13, 17, 18, 29, 50, 58
Post-Capitalist Transition 3, 21, 56, 60–61
prefigurative politics 23
public-civic partnerships 26

regulation of digital commons 55, 60
renewable energy and cooperatives 9, 10
resilience in cooperative economies 16, 23, 34, 36

smart cities and digital commons 34, 41, 43
social economy and commons 26, 30
solidarity economy 22, 24, 26, 39, 41, 42
sustainability in open cooperativism 1–5, 11, 12, 16, 22, 23, 27, 28, 30, 33, 34, 38, 41, 50, 51, 54–58, 60

technological sovereignty 28
thematic analysis of cooperatives 4, 53–56
transition economics 8, 16, 42, 52, 56, 60, 61

Universal Basic Income (UBI) 2, 4, 29, 44, 55

value proposition of cooperatives 3, 4, 30, 41, 56, 57, 58, 59
venture capital and cooperatives 23

workers' cooperatives 12

Zero Marginal Cost Society 9

www.ingramcontent.com/pod-product-compliance
Lightning Source LLC
LaVergne TN
LVHW100921110826
845155LV00035B/44

* 9 7 8 1 8 0 1 3 6 0 9 9 9 *